CALIFORNIA:

WALKING THROUGH CHANGE

Explore California from
Shasta to Joshua Tree

BILL ROZDAY

Potomac Pages

Frederick, Maryland

CALIFORNIA: WALKING THROUGH CHANGE
Bill Rozday
Potomac Pages
Frederick, Maryland

Copyright 2022 by Bill Rozday

Published by
POTOMAC PAGES
6671 Seagull Court, Frederick, MD 21703
www.potomacpages.net

The author or publisher assumes no responsibility for the impact of
any outdoor-related activities undertaken in response to this book.

Printed in the United States of America
First Edition: December 2022

Book Design by KarrieRoss.com
Cover Photo by Bill Rozday
Petroglyph icon from author photo, Lava Beds National Monument
Publisher's Cataloging-in-Publication
Rozday, Bill
California: Walking Through Change – First Edition
pages.cm
Includes index.

ISBN   9798366420341

Hiking—United States—Guidebooks. 2.   Natural history—United States—
Guidebooks. Mountain plants—United States—Guidebooks. 4. Mountain
animals—United States—Guidebooks.   5.   United States—Guidebooks.
I. Title

For the California Believers

Other Books by Bill Rozday

Hikes in High Places

High Ground

Peak Hikes of the Mid-Atlantic States

High Ground II

Hiking Appalachian Topographic Culture

High Ground III

Freedom Hikes

Preface

High Ground

California is America's outstanding interface of people and nature. The statistics affirm it: at least 45,000,000 acres of public land over which 38,000,000 residents roam freely.

So how do the people make use of their rough 1 acre per capita, this showcase dividend of democracy? Appropriately, it's the everyday person who visits it most often. Certainly, a class of high-tech adventurers bike, backpack and climb it, but the overwhelming majority walk over their acre as their backyard, admiring it and wondering at its history. Whether First Nations, immigrant farmers, ranchers, they embody the evolution of man-earth relations in California.

They come here walking through their own changes – from Mexico, from the Philippines, from across the earth. If you could have met the people I have met struggling to build their lives as they walked these high paths, you could never feel dismissiveness or apathy again.

These are sites where the man-earth evolution took place and continues today. They are cliffs, summits, ledges, hills. They are our high ground, democracy's back yard.

Contents

CALIFORNIA:
WALKING THROUGH CHANGE

CHAPTER 1

Headlands

MENDOCINO

(*Pomo Nation*)
Elevation 154

Mendocino Headlands Fragrance restored me at some point after a 2:00 a.m. drive into a black Northern Pacific emptiness. I stepped into the early April morning as the sun, cresting the hilltop town behind me like crystal, touched a Headlands wet with spring dew. The remarkable diversity and density of grasses breathed a self-sustaining fragrance – not mower-induced, but offered freely. Each step was a distillation of Mendocino Headlands.

The unexpected fragrance of The Headlands answers the contrarian layout of the town behind them. Their empty grasses occupy the closest foot-falls to the Pacific, where villas and cottages should be rather than the diminishing progression of wood palings halting a quarter of a mile back. My walk led among an intuitive network of informal paths commencing where antique streets faded out.

Framing it was arguably the most glorious landscape on Earth, created by a Pacific Ocean that asserts its presence forcefully. Sea arches lend a ragged contour to the frame. To the south, to the north, to the west, the aquamarine waves rush through them, wetting the deep green kelp covering the rock, romping carelessly.

A bizarre void opened at my feet. I looked down through the earth itself to the sound of ocean. The sea pierced the Headlands, surging over 150 feet below the grass through a hole that long-lost redwood (*Sequoia sempervirens*) loggers used to slide tree trunks through to a waiting ship.

Over countless ancient mornings, complex geology achieved the tremendous table of earth here on which we work out a scheme of botanical cooperation. It involved change so deep and broad that it overcame the ocean itself. Before the redwood forest cloaking the Headlands yielded to the settlements that took advantage of its high flatness, it was a wet slab of sand washed by tides.

The slab disappeared beneath the ice of a continental glacier, which maintained it in a position above the Pacific by lowering the sea water around it as it took up the saltwater into the glacial structure. A powerful earthquake then elevated the table further, far enough upward that subsequent glacial melting left it above the rising sea level, in the sheet outline that the ice pressed.

First Nations people appropriated the headlands along this segment of the Pacific coast as a fishing ground. North of Mendocino, a projecting table of land lies with vegetation nearly polished away from their footfalls made while preparing their mussel and abalone harvest, a steep mountainside behind them and beneath them the surf.

Mendocino Headlands Fragrance is a result of a giving back and forth between nature and man. As Portuguese farmers tilled the land, they created space for native grasses to flourish freely and convey April through their scent. Wildflowers such as yellow poppies and indian paintbrush accompanied the grasses and maintained a dialogue with the sun. The Portuguese also brought Mediterranean grasses with them, which seeded themselves and mingled with the native varieties, importing Europe to the migrant farmers.

Chinese settlers maintained plant relations that transferred to the Headlands. Above Portuguese Beach in spring, the yellow-flowering kale the Chinese introduced brightens the foreground of the town portraits that photographers shoot.

The Headlands remained a zone of open grass because the Mendocino founders avoided the Portuguese immigrants farming its soil, unaware that nature was cloaking such prejudice with an exemplary prairie. As the redwood shacks of the newcomers deteriorated, the land fell into disuse and the county acquired it. What started as class exclusion eventually led in 1974 to the inclusive designation of State Park for the 347-acre Headlands. Now, the strong ocean that carried diverse people to Mendocino exerts its influence through the prevailing winds blowing inland from the ocean, knitting exotic and native grasses into a prairie grass library.

At Mendocino Headlands, on possibly the most picturesque high ground on earth, we meet and we look now. The logging and farming and ocean harvesting are through. Much as the land here settled itself after the earthquake lifted it, our culture has rearranged itself. It has settled into a diverse community of painters, photographers, poets that echoes the ethnic diversity drawn from this land. The paths it follows run through the grasses of the most magnificent cultural backyard in America.

PROFILE

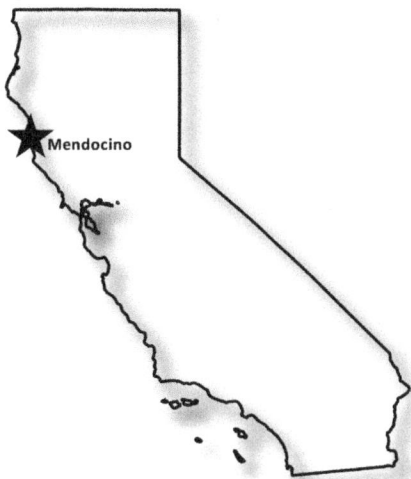

Trip Outline: San Francisco – CA-101 north 85 miles – CA 128-W 55 miles – CA 1-N north 10 miles

Difficulty: 1 of 10
Length: .05 miles
Elevation Change: 0
Water: Yes
Toilets: Yes
Surface: Grass/Dirt

Best time of year: May, after the cold and wind at this high latitude subsides and the wildflowers start blooming

Along the trail: Sheltered Portuguese Beach and restaurants on Main Street

*Hazards: Steep descents from Headlands to surf;
poison oak in unkempt areas near town*

CHAPTER 2

Promontory

CARMEL-BY-THE-SEA

(*Ohlone Nation*)
Elevation 167

*O*f all earthen footfalls, none could be more provocative. At Point Lobos, two globally rare, picturesque species of conifer roof the trail, and the impact points of ocean and human vision are incomparable. Then the monarch butterflies come and turn the depths of winter orange at this northern head of California's Big Sur.

Closest Big Sur outpost to heavy traffic, at Carmel-by-the-Sea, lacking the mountain aesthetics to the south, Point Lobos State Natural Reserve is civilized Big Sur, a technical boundary, but its scenery is counter-technical – theatrical. I first visited this place intending to photograph winter mushrooms. On the transforming interface of the Cypress Grove Trail, Point Lobos became a soft mushroom cap of eloquent land atop the stem of a Pacific promontory.

It returned me to childhood days. Footfalls were soft and obstruction-free. Here the ocean crashed behind wind-graced tree outlines; there it crashed again; there at a third commanding angle, again. The light falls in shafts, as through the classic frosted pane of a grade school classroom. Fragrant cypress logs stacked by the trail-keeper summon the remembered scent of pencils in the still and humid shadows. Fanciful pencil wood to be sure, these Monterey cypresses (*Hesperocyparis macrocarpa*) grow nowhere else on earth. I hear a long-lost teacher telling me not to lose my pencils for the field trip.

The word "Monterey" identifies county, peninsula, cypress, and Monterey pine (*Pinus radiata*) as well. The field trip ascends into those pines, which appear endless even though their rarity is nearly as extreme as that of the cypresses, with only three natural occurrences on the planet. Point Lobos is a point of misleading abundance.

We are going to a quiet place to see pieces of orange stained glass and to watch them come to life as monarch butterfly wings. Hundreds of stained glass wings move in a kind of flutter that denotes an event within the flitting linear journey of butterfly migration. The wings multiply. The fluttering graces pine needles dangling with moss, the washed blue of Pacific sky as backdrop.

This forest has hosted the flutter dance for thousands of years. The character-filled topography of the Point Lobos coves features slopes sheltered from ocean wind where the air remains mild. Point Lobos is the entry point of an indented Big Sur coastline that stretches for nearly 100 miles and provides 7 flutter sites for wintering monarchs. Like the Monterey pine, the monarchs lend an idyllic but illusionary quality of abundance to the landscape.

The social reality is that wherever the people of the Pacific coast migrate to, they tend to carry with them the exchange scheme of monarch butterflies for manicured lawn. The fragrant, uncouth jumble of milkweeds essential to monarch reproduction has disappeared from untold thousands of sites, can-celling out new butterfly generations.

A cultural equation illustrates the issue: x feet of unmown yard or fencerow = a monarch flutter on this sea-sheltered hillside. Do we tend our life's lawn with precisely identical strokes, our vision absolutely level, or look upward for these memo-rable moments?

Nearby Pacific Grove and Carmel-by-the-Sea look upward, demonstrating the links between cre-ativity and conservation. Local author and musician Alex Krysyna talks of the butterfly bush plantings that sustain the celebrated monarch population at Monastery Beach, which features a backdrop of music from the monastery. This beach, adjacent to Point Lobos, features a grove of eucalyptus trees covered with orange wings each winter. The road-side leading past Point Lobos itself overflows with hundreds of cars from monarch watchers exceeding the Reserve's visitation limits and following a beach path there in California's premier example of spontaneous nature appreciation.

Even if monarch butterflies were accorded official "protection," their only true protection would come from our personal revolts against technological rule. We have to want to pick blackberries in the weeds. We have to want to blow milkweed seeds in the wind. We have to believe there is this place as beautiful as a video game, because there is, but so few believed it that the orange wings that fluttered in the Monterey pine of the Reserve vanished in 2021.

PROFILE

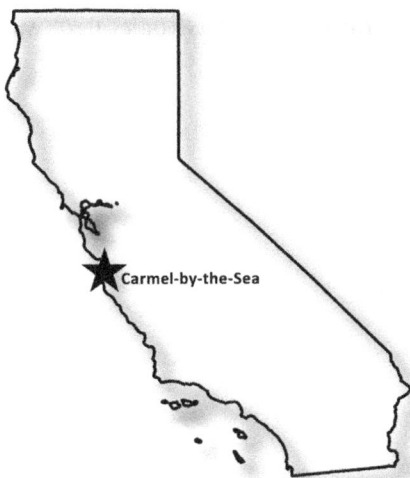

*Trip Outline: San Francisco – CA 101-S 116 miles—
CA 1-S 5 miles — Carmel-by-the-Sea – East on
Ocean Avenue 0.7 miles – CA 1-S 3.4 miles*

*Difficulty: 1 of 10
Length: 1.0 miles
Elevation change: 100
Water: Yes
Toilets: Yes
Surface: Grass/dirt*

*Best time of year: December, to correspond with the
monarch butterfly migration. Seals, marine birds
and deer make this, along with Joshua Tree, the rich-
est faunal experience of any of the 20 hikes.*

Along the trail: Educational material and park per-sonnel

Hazards: Poison oak and dangerous rocks near surf

CHAPTER 3

Cliff Edge

GORDA

(Salinan/Chumash Nations)
Elevation 325

T *he Indians knew all the cool places*, Cindy, Ragged Point Inn gift shop manager, told me. Her voice trailed off wistfully.

The resort's restaurant is adjacent, and I was savoring the Small Stack of gourmet pancakes one morning. As I poured maple syrup, sun beat down through the glass ceiling amidst the wood beams and stone. Dining there is at once indoor and outdoor. Waiting for me in the sea-washed air through the abundant glass behind the outdoor tables was an exhibit of modern/ancient fusion. It was a lesson offered in an outdoor classroom leading to a superb Pacific view.

Four circular holes pocked a hard serpentine outcropping jutting above the manicured lawn and garden path. Called "grinding holes," not uncommon here yet largely unknown to tourists, they formed as native Americans ground foodstuffs. Right there along Route 1, I found the California spirit, that lost and longed-for earth connection.

Anthropological research at Cal-Poly in San Luis Obispo established the Ragged Point grinding holes as Salinan in origin. Such sites can be as recent as 150 years or can be much, much older. The Salinans who fashioned them were a division of the tribe called Playano – "beach people" – by Spanish explorers. Salinan villages stretched from Morro Rock to Dolan Rock, Salinas to Cuesta Grade Summit, and as far as 70 miles eastward to the Diablo Range, Temblor Range and the Painted Rock of Carrizo Plain. Today the Salinan Nation, which once numbered 3,000 souls, consists of about 800.

Salinan Tribal Administrator Patti Dunton explained how the tribe "mapped" the territory of the beach people. Their map was one of existential poetry: a Western Gate facing a Great Fire.

I wondered if the Salinans were making acorn pancakes 1,000 years ago out back of the resort restaurant. They ground this staple in these rock mortars and then leached out the tannin in water, producing an acorn meal that they baked into cakes.

I learned the complex lore of these grinding holes when Tribal Chair John Burch honored me with his insights on Ragged Point. That outcropping was actually a long-ago organic kitchen counter. "Tegula shellfish were as important a food as acorns," he explained, as I recalled the whorled snails washed up on the Big Sur beach below. "They ground them up shell and all and mixed them with acorns or other meats." Their high salt content not only lent food flavor but preserved their tiny meats on long journeys. "They ground herbs there," he told me as well. As hunter-gatherers, they made use of unusual foods such as tree lichens.

Then John Burch told me the age of the Ragged Point rock mortars.

Whatever they were grinding, they ground it long ago – 10,000 years ago. He could tell the age by the convex form of the mortars, created in an ancient process employing a wooden implement. They first broke the rock apart with an agate drill and then smoothed the contours through the circular grinding motion. He reminded me that this mortar site, when in use, was a clifftop 25 miles inland from the ocean. It was still a cool place, but bereft of crashing ocean sound, which approached over the intervening ages. Time tends to smooth over boundaries.

These days, as Tribal Chair, John Burch deals with the politics of boundaries. The ancient neighbors of the Salinans, the Chumash to the south, overlapped with the Salinans around Ragged Point. The Salinans objected to Ragged Point's inclusion in the proposed Chumash Heritage National Marine Sanctuary on the grounds that millennia ago, Salinans packed shellfish on foot over the Chumash sanctuary's seabed, dry land at the time.

The grinding holes behind the restaurant establish the clifftop as Salinan, but the Chair prefers to look at it in an older way. "It doesn't matter whether those grinding holes were Chumash or Salinan," he says. "What matters is that they offer a window into learning." Through the Ragged Point Inn restaurant windows, I looked out at a 10,000-year-old kitchen classroom facing a Great Fire.

A brief walk at Ragged Point leads through resort gardens to the "point" itself, an arrowhead of land overlooking the sea at a cliff edge. Since the path leads over the secure grounds of the resort, it offers the unusual opportunity for a nighttime hike.

We read often of "dark sky" zones in the desert, but little of the deep oceanside darkness. On that high ragged point, rushing downslope wind offsets a coffee table atlas of constellations.

Invisible in the shadows but white by day, a huge grinding rock points to the ocean. A hundreds-ton Ragged Point, its cupped grinding mark silent above the surf and wind noise, it answers the sense of perspective the night sky presents, part of real California where native Pacific culture remains with us, waiting to see what transpires in the next 10,000 years.

Among the carefully curated gifts arrayed at the Ragged Point gift shop, crude and ancient rocks drape over decorative driftwood. The green and gray of mossy tree bark, they dangle from leather thongs. They signal something that the jade plants of the dining room décor answer. They are jade pieces, and their signal emanates from far below on the beach: Salinans wielding jade to hammer abalone shells open with it for sustenance and pre-California abalone jewelry capital.

A 1964 anthropology dissertation from Cal-Berkeley interprets the discovery of dozens of jade hammerstones along this beach in 1951/52. This was at a place called Willow Creek.

I emerge in wet January grayness and drive north 9 miles to a surfside parking space, a thousands-foot mountainside and long vacation journey jutting behind me. 2,400 flight miles and 240 rental car miles dissolve through meditation before I comb Jade Beach. Standing on the edge of it, I look long and hard at my surroundings, situating myself carefully within them. This surveying of the shore, this stage, is the anticipation of discovery. Then my feet touch the beach.

I set about doing what seemingly everyone does on Jade Beach – look for jade pebbles.

Jade Beach, formally known as Willow Creek Beach, is part of central California's Big Sur, a 100-mile stretch of unspoiled coastline between Carmel-by-the-Sea and Cambria. Willow Creek, a crystal mountain stream worked heavily during the Gold Rush era, divides it into North and South designations, while a 3-4-foot tide regulates access.

At the basic level, what I do on Jade Beach is hunting and gathering, one of the most mentally calming of human pursuits and a universal practice. Some human beings hunt mushrooms, some hunt pine cones, some wildflowers, all seeking the mental absorption that these activities offer. Hunting jade here by the Pacific, the audial massage of surf and ancient mythos of the stone amplify the effects.

A subculture of Jade Beach jade hunters uses its finds to fill vases, create jewelry, or in the case of more substantial discoveries, as massage stones. They proclaim membership in the tribe by wearing their finds as pendants on leather thongs. Patience and perception earn the coveted inclusion, and the first discovery can bring wide eyes and excited tones to the most well-traveled. They meet each October at the widely attended Big Sur Jade Festival (69325 Highway 1, Big Sur, CA 93920).

Combing the rocky coves, out of cell phone range, my mind enters the final, crucial stage of change: the shedding of objectives, digits, instant gratification. Maybe one of 1,000 wave-polished stones is jade. Jade hunters don't count stones. Counting to the thousandth would render the hunt a maddening exercise when it is the exact opposite if practiced properly. I merge with the environment, appraise a piece of redwood driftwood. Then, I celebrate a rainbow fragment of abalone shell. I know that the jade is coming.

Jade Beach withheld the gem from me for years, during which I learned to focus on stones that felt heavy in my hands or possessed a certain gleam.

After one trip, I submitted a screenshot of such a stone, patterned in a beach dualism of seafoam-white and cliffside-black, to local jade master and former jade miner Kenny Comello, who returned a thrilling "nice score," affirming that jade hunting was not an entirely green matter and was also as much tactile as visual.

Geologic ages ago, an offshore subduction zone produced an earthquake that pushed the coastal plate against the native rock of the Santa Lucia Mountains at Jade Beach. The unimaginable stress merged minerals and created the gem in a planetary transformation. The force of surf breaks off pieces and washes them, polished, ashore. No other beach on earth holds this nephrite jade.

The discovery of jade is not a given here. What is a given is that the mind will be healed before it is discovered.

I have walked this beach a few hours at a time over a period of 10 years and learned not only about jade but subjects equally elusive. A primary tenet of the man-nature bond is discovering all by focusing on one place over a long period.

2017: I rounded the corner of the sharp cliff on North Jade Beach and sat down with several huge elephant seals occupying the dark sand. Had I recognized then their bad attitude and ability to outrun a human on a beach, I would have moved on before sitting down. Their usual habitat was 25 miles south, where a tourist boardwalk protects people and the

10-foot, 2000-pound animals from each other. These rebel seals decided to "haul out" here instead.

2020: I arrived at North Jade Beach at dawn and trudged past the cliff corner once more. I relished the emptiness of the sands, unblemished by fellow hunters, but then saw an extended line of animal prints. They were the webbed footfalls of a sea otter, and the tracks were a rare sight, evidence of an unusual episode causing the almost exclusively aquatic creature to hit the beach.

The individual greens of jade, answering the green waves, satisfy, but my fellow jade-seekers also validate my pursuit. On one excursion, a surfer in a black wetsuit tossed me a jet-black piece gleaming like glass; continuing across Willow Creek, I found a solitary beach bum scrubbing a stone furiously, bringing out hidden green, talking excitedly about marks on it made by indigenous people – still talking, no doubt.

What discovery comes next for me on Jade Beach? What rarity awaits? All rarities await there for surfers and beach bums alike.

Then my trip ends in a maze of 12 Rental Car Return arrows forcing me to a shadowed parking space at SFO. I clear the car of my valuables and, still holding onto Jade Beach, hand a green pebble to the attendant, who inspects it with her Eastern eyes and returns a smile. We acknowledge that both of us came from a place far away.

PROFILE

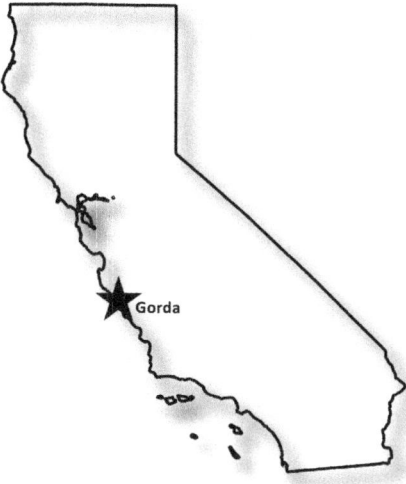

Trip Outline: Los Angeles – CA 101-N 97 miles – CA 154-W 34 miles — CA 101-N 57 miles – CA 1-N 25 miles

Difficulty: 0 of 10
Length: 0.25 miles
Elevation Change: 0
Water: Yes
Toilets: Yes
Surface: Gravel

Best time of year: October, after the summer period of heavy morning mists

Along the trail: Expertly tended gardens, excellent restaurant and gift shop

Hazards: None along this trail, but caution necessary while driving and beach-walking this stretch of coast. The forces that shape the spectacular topography continually work to create immense landslides and anomalous waves. Bear in mind the absence of cell phone coverage along Jade Beach.

CHAPTER 4

Vista

VENTURA

(*Chumash Nation*)
Elevation 743

*P*ossibly the most visible natural symbol in the state caps a hill directly above California 101-N. Crowning the Coast Range backing the city of Ventura, a pair of prominent trees illustrate a saga of high topography dating to 1898. The arboreal narrative features law, weather and geography in one of America's most notable relations with high ground.

Southern California is noticeably bereft of trees, with its mountains sun-drenched cartographic outlines. Whether widely spaced grassland oaks or white California sycamores along the rare watercourses, individual trees command greater attention, becoming friends of sorts.

The 1898 planting of 13 non-native blue gum eucalyptus on the hilltop sowed a lasting high ground bond with the earth here. the city along the Pacific below grew from an agricultural area centered around a Spanish hacienda and Mexican adobe to a major population center, the two trees standing stark on the barren ridgeline continued their oversight and residents retained their regard for them, hiking regularly to them to pay their respects. Hiking was a part of the Ventura social fabric long before it transitioned into a commercial sport and spread from west to east across the country. Two Trees became Ventura's symbol and reflection of the California mindset.

The eucalyptus pair acquired the title Two Trees as various challenges to their existence arose: brushfire, vandalism. The original 13 trees that formed their small grove fluctuated in size, finally reduced to two, a 116-year-old and a 58-year-old, by 2014, when they first gave me pause through the windshield glass.

A receptive non-native, I recognized an educational opportunity on the hill. I saw that the sharpness of the ascent to the trees is an emblem of the near-constant presence of steep terrain in the state. The tan dust that rises with each step betrays the dry climate that decimated the grove with fire, while the long history of hikes to this summit shows the simple love of nature of Californians. From Two Trees, the high ground offers a significant view of the seacoast city exchanging tree and resort beach vistas, as well as the distinctive Channel Island landforms rising dark in the haze.

A haven of peace ever since early days when they appeared on sailing charts as mariner guideposts, their bond with the city frayed amidst ownership dispute and regulations until the Rancho Ventura Conservation Trust, founded in 2016 by Richard Atmore, restored their security. A brief period of transition during which hikes to the trees were illegal and natural disasters visited their ridgeline gave way to a management plan for 860 acres of surrounding land and restoration of hiking privileges.

Two Trees illustrates a healthy pairing of practical and idealistic land preservation. The active oversight of the Trust combats threats from invasive plants and wildfire/erosion cycles while maintaining its use as a working cattle ranch, returning it to early days of a more congenial man/earth relationship.

Episodes of destruction and renewal overtook the ridgeline in the second decade of the 21st century. A windstorm felled the dead trunk of the last legacy tree, the 116-year-old, and then the great Thomas Fire of 2017 charred its prostrate remains. A replacement tree ceremony for the 116-year-old reset the pairing of Two Trees and renewed their bond with Ventura The happy gathering spread a green awareness east across America as the eucalyptus pair rejoined the Ventura symbols of Spanish mission and Mexican adobe.

For educational hikes to Two Trees, contact Rancho Ventura Conservation Trust at http://www.ventura-conservation.com or 805-644-6850.

PROFILE

Ventura

*Trip Outline: Los Angeles – CA 101-N 68 miles –
Foothill Road 2 miles*

Difficulty: 6 of 10
Length: 3.0 miles
Elevation change: 716
Water: No
Toilets: Yes
Surface: Grass/dirt

*Best time of year: October, after the intense heat and
dryness of summer subsides*

*Along the trail: An interpretive guide provides
information on the history and ecology of Two
Trees and their environs. Contact Rancho Ventura*

Conservation Trust at http://www.venturaconserva-tion.com or 805-644-6850.

Hazards: Aside from California's ubiquitous poison oak and the unlikely rattlesnake sighting, none. The guide oversees your progress.

CHAPTER 5

Hilltop

CASTRO VALLEY

(Ohlone Nation)
Elevation 808

Behind Castro Valley, California, a city of hill-side streets, rise hills with a different identity – hills of a bordering nature, pale and barren like an eloquently fashioned wall, bereft of even the most minor straggling house or road. I climbed atop them into their grasses and felt within me the gravity of their border.

These San Leandro Hills, part of the California Coast Ranges, are the initial high ground beyond the Hayward-San Leandro earthquake fault line lying silent in the flat town of Hayward spread out beneath their grassy rim. They wrinkle and pitch with the look of violence that has ceased, covered over.

Perpetual strife beneath them, hikers on Fairmont Ridge look upward. On America's western border, the old Atlantic grayness behind, they leave their own border marks.

At the base of the ridge, in the city of Hayward itself, a juvenile correctional institution stands within the earthquake fault zone and its incipient wedge of destruction. Overseeing its violent divisions with peace, a monument to children killed by violence crowns the hill. Rows of symbolic trees, one planted per year, rise behind the polished granite.

The full view of San Francisco, altered by Bay mists, stands in the distance below the overseeing clarity of the hilltop. In the Bay, WWII threats resounded in the hilltop eucalyptus in a military post later abandoned as reason transcended conflict. Here on this restful patio of land, we watch the fog and fault lines.

We leave our marks and look upward. Their natural habitat thousands of miles away, some of the first eucalyptus trees brought to America took root on this hill in the 1860s. Tall and white-trunked, a row of them occupies the crest. With no forest to accompany them and only sky above, we made the eucalyptus row the fragrant border of the cities of Castro Valley and Hayward. Beside them runs the cart tracks of a pioneer road now supplanted with the prints of caring thoughts. On the San Francisco-Washington, D.C. flight path, the eucalyptus row runs as a window seat landmark.

The bent pockets of hilltop hold memorials. Across the narrow ridge line from the grassy rim above Hayward is the overlook of Lake Chabot; standing amidst the summer gold is a bench dedicated to a hiker who regarded the lake below from this view before crossing the border of this life.

The signs we leave on the land are often borders, and borders denote the value of things being divided. On the gold grasslands of these California Coast Ranges, looking across the San Francisco Bay and an old world left behind across the Pacific, stone walls of unknown origin run.

The identity of the abandoned Old World is unknown. Speculation includes unrecorded Chinese wall-builders landing on our shore thousands of years ago. Maybe it is our First Nations peoples' old world abandoned at its western front when meted out and structured as pastureland by the Spanish. Along the ridgeline foundation, the earth's mass strays like broken mushroom caps picked up and set in order, the wind playing unhindered through the grass between provocative mountain and water view.

From high points like Mission Peak, where the San Leandro Hills fill out into the Diablo Range, over 100 miles of beyond, including the Sierra Nevada mountains, is visible from the crest, a vastness which modern scientists measure as a "viewshed," an atmospheric resource.

As I walked beneath the arid sky of the San Leandro Hills, a flock of Western bluebirds (*Sialia mexicana*) – wild, yet not wild – flitted across the free and unkempt yard of the hilltop. Neither sober illustrations in a birder's field guide nor city sparrows;

divested of the gloomy legends of their eastern cousins portending death as they fly against windows, they were the blue-sky border of grasses, the happy brightness of day, the setting of an upward-directed healing point.

Golden in the April-to-November drought and green in the remaining months of winter rains, tended by cattle as they have long been between successive earthquakes, the hills behind Castro Valley are a bicolored blanket. The early settlers grazed cows and goats on this ridge of quieted upheaval, following economically the First Nations people with their hilltop hunts; now, the cattle graze for a social purpose. Today, a herd of goats advances this humble use of the hills by grazing during the season of alien grass growth, then moving on when the parks department determines that the native purple needlegrass (*Nassella pulchra*) that originally clothed these hills begins to sprout.

From the jurisdictional border of the eucalyptus trees, the owls perch in motionless division of night and day. They leave a friendly feather on the ground and a few cries but are only the border between the seen and unseen. Owls gone, the day begins and the hikers in the San Leandro Hills transcend, traversing the wild and yet-not-wild yard within a fold of night and day, green winter and gold summer.

PROFILE

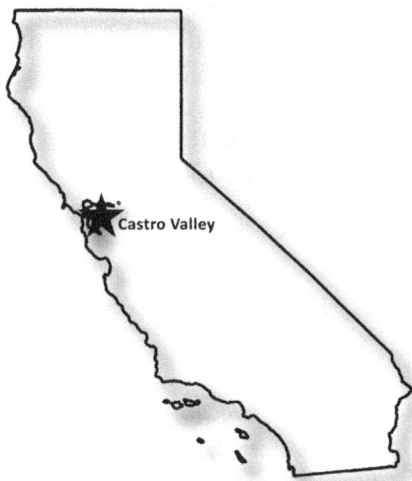

Trip Outline: San Francisco – CA 580-E – Castro Valley Highway 1 mile – Lake Chabot Road 2 miles – Small lot upslope from Lake Chabot entrance

Difficulty: 3 of 10
Length: 1.0 miles
Elevation change: 300
Water: Yes
Toilets: Yes
Surface: Grass/dirt

Best time of year: May to October, after the rainy season ends

Along the trail: Urban perspectives balanced with idyllic open space; lunch available at the nearby entrance to Lake Chabot. A hike during summer here means a hike during fire season, with regular fire engine patrols. Nearby, the Oakland Firestorm of 1991, accelerated by the rugged terrain and flammable eucalyptus foliage, claimed 25 lives.

Hazards: Aside from the ever-present poison oak and the rare rattlesnake sighting, none to speak of

CHAPTER 6

High Pass

LIVERMORE

(*Ohlone Nation*)
Elevation 1010

*T*wo air currents of planetary scale, Pacific Ocean Westerly and Central Valley Thermal, meet at Altamont Pass, one hour east of San Francisco, to support one of America's largest wind farms and densest populations of golden eagles. The dual currents permit the wind farm to supply the burgeoning Bay Area with electric power and supply golden eagles the moving air in which they carry on a hunting tradition spanning thousands of generations.

Wind moves at an average 15 miles per hour through the pass, which stands at an altitude of 1,010 feet, while the wrinkled Coast Range that the pass splits offers a complex pattern of canyons and hills populated by California ground squirrels (*Otospermophilus beecheyi*), chief food of the nesting eagles. These conditions support roughly 200 pairs of nesting eagles and a further influx of winter migrants, with 4930 wind turbines arrayed in dead-ly opposition.

Hans Peters, Professor Emeritus of biology at neighboring Chabot College, offers a startling insight on the singularity of this habitat. The density of golden eagle nests within the 50,000-acre tract between Mts. Diablo and Hamilton, landmark summits bordering the Altamont Wind Farm, approaches 1 nest per half-mile at some points, whereas a typical separation distance for the species is at least 15 miles. This eagle congregation nests in the groves of California live oak (*Quercus agrifolia*) that cloak the scheme of steep slopes, preferring north-facing ground.

Brushy Peak Regional Park, outside of Livermore, provides a close look at the picturesque live oak trees that host the golden eagles and define this Mediterranean landscape. The rocky ground and strong winds limit their height, producing wide canopies of shadow that combine with their dark evergreen foliage to create a "brushy" appearance from a distance.

Those factors also limit their utility as wood, resulting in very old specimens dotting the grass-lands. The flat rocks and sheltering foliage created a day-use resort for picnickers long ago, and the temptation to sit under the oaks persists, affirmed by informal paths leading under them where the Brushy Peak Loop Trail reaches its highest point.

The surrounding winds create a sense of solitude here. Often at 30-40 mph, they rush through the oaks with a sound like surf and rattle the brittle grasses. Our efficient wind turbines follow in their imperfect way the reliable currents generating this solitude of eagles. The wind turbines perform their work silently, detracting little from the viewshed. At the Laughlin Ranch Staging Area, where hikes begin, a draw runs to the base of hills crowned with white blades.

Illustration: Julie Parker, Paso Robles, California

The birds launch into the Altamont Airshed, their wings fixed upon prey, locked into air currents, as the blades of wind turbines lock in a spin. The resultant meeting of 100-mph wings and 200-mph blades sacrificed about 70 eagles per year before conservation groups and energy companies entered into studies of the dueling air currents and eagle wings.

In 2021, East Bay Community Energy announced the replacement of 569 outdated wind turbines with 23 higher-tech structures positioned nearly 500 feet above ground level. Their studies suggested a typical bird flight elevation below the 500-foot level.

The reduction in the number of turbines clears air space of technology-bird encounters; combined with other measures, it reduces total bird loss. Siting the new turbines away from nesting areas and eliminating nearby power lines aids further in reducing the number of annual eagle casualties to around 18.

On this high pass, golden eagles showed us the unity of air and land. In our partnership, we picked up their sacrificed forms from Altamont, donated their feathers for native American ceremonies, and molded our technologies into wings.

PROFILE

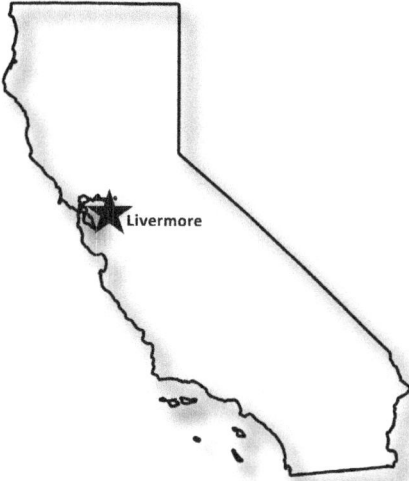

Trip Outline: San Francisco – I 80-E 8 miles – I 580-E 37 miles – North Vasco Road 6 miles –Laughlin Road 2 miles

Difficulty: 7 of 10
Length: 3.0 miles
Elevation change: 500
Water: Yes
Toilets: Yes
Surface: Dirt/rock

Best time of year: May/June, before the wildflowers and grasses fade away

Along the trail: Sweeping views of grassy hills bordering the East Bay; picturesque resting spots with flat rocks beneath spreading oak branches

Hazards: Slippery rock surfaces and dehydrating winds

CHAPTER 7

Upthrust Fault

SOLEDAD

(Ohlone Nation)
Elevation 1200

It was a good place for giant vultures. The California condor (*Gymnogyps californianus*) attains a 9.5-foot wingspan and can approach 20 pounds in weight; yet, when it soars on the rushing winds, it becomes a solitary avian athlete, reaching speeds of 55 miles per hour. Climbing high on the thermal currents, into the domain of airplanes, its straightly held wings and white-marked underside ruffle in the atmosphere up to 15,000 feet above these canyons and pines.

It was a hostile place where the dry heat immediately drew all the moisture from my nose, startling me. The vegetation stood silent, with only the sound of the dessicating wind above. Manzanita shrubs bled a maroon color along the trail beneath the condor's sky.

To the condor, Pinnacles National Park represents a high ground reference point amidst thermal currents. As the winds rise skyward, a nesting bird flaps off of a high rock and into its hunting environment of dry air and heat, searching for the fallen animal life below. It selects the most elevated habitat, lending its own functional definition to the idea of high ground.

The condors were up there on their unique piece of high ground. This surpassing vulture species was waging a comeback in numbers on rocks that constituted an ancient volcano. The movement of an earthquake fault line transferred the volcano many miles from its origin; then, millions of years of erosion fashioned the intricate rock palace that the birds now called home – a temple of geologic struggle.

Condors inhabited Pinnacles historically, but human persecution reduced their numbers to a point near extinction, with the last recorded fly-over by a wild bird in 1987. Shortly thereafter, every bird remaining in the wild had its wildness suspended as biologists bred the condors in controlled conditions and then released them into the rock-bedded atmosphere of the California mountains.

This last sailing condor was likely AC9, Adult Condor 9, on a long-distance flight through its range searching for fellow condors. In the spring of 1987, researchers captured AC9 and subsequently bred it in captivity. In 2002, they released it in Ventura County, restoring a wilderness time clock suspended for 15 years, during which time they saved the species from impending extinction.

The place represented an isolated enclave of high ground attended by a winged high ground element. The approach road, CA-25, penetrated the secluded and sparse San Andreas Rift Zone, a Mexican-like valley of heat and farms, and then found itself encroached upon by narrowing topographic walls, forcing it to slow and wind before it reached the shaded canyon floor with its gift shop and information center.

A naturalist in the rear of the center studied a remote camera to monitor the progress of condor chicks in a nest far above. The birds were off-limits to visitors during this sensitive stage of life, but a ranger near a research station up in the rocks tracked condor movements, and hikers were prowling the ridgetop trying to learn of their whereabouts.

It was a day of motionless views of the Gabilan Mountains east of the Salinas Valley, a place of pause and uncertainty. There was scant green on the top of this earthquake-transported volcano's top, little in the way of life. It was a place of a powerful bird that suggested a time without the trees and fields and homes we know today. It was as though millions of empty years perched on the sandstone peaks.

Established in 1908 by Theodore Roosevelt, Pinnacles contains 26,000 acres, of which 16,000 are designated as wilderness. Over 30 miles of hiking trails traverse the resistant landscape of rock and rattlesnakes, and I stood there then along one of them, letting the distinctive surroundings reflect on me.

I searched out the meaning of the desolation. More than a National Park but a Monument of Eons, Pinnacles was there long before human beings came to this earth. It was an elevated custodian of the life that was present in this region, sending these winged emissaries to dine on the animals that died their natural deaths between these formations and the Pacific Ocean. All of this living, all of these laughing people, have not succeeded in embellishing the facelessness of this ancient crest and the death-seeking wings that soar from it.

PROFILE

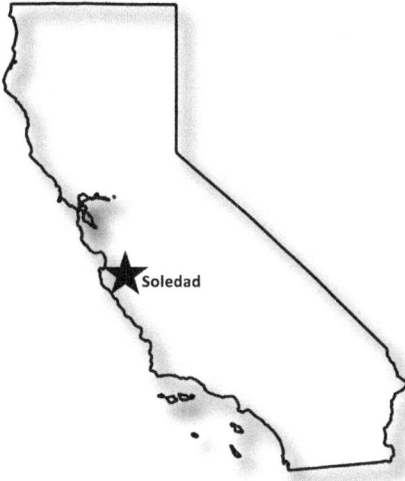

Trip Outline: San Francisco – CA 101-S 79 miles – Gilroy — CA 25-S 30 miles – CA 146-E 5 miles – Bear Gulch Visitor Center

Difficulty: 9 of 10
Length: 3 miles
Elevation Change: 1100
Water: Yes
Toilets: Yes
Surface: Dirt/stone
Best time of year: October to May, outside of the season of extreme heat

Along the trail: The Bear Gulch Visitor Center provides parking, shade, and park personnel

Hazards: Rattlesnakes favor this rocky expanse and the cliffs and outcroppings present hazards to footing. If visiting during the warm months, time your hike for the morning for the best chance to view condors and avoid the debilitating heat.

CHAPTER 8

Viewshed

CAMBRIA

(*Chumash Nation*)
Elevation 1700

Stunning natural beauty typically shies away from highway pavement, but at one simple pull-off along one highway in central California, mere steps lead to a full embrace.

Illustration: Nolan Henderson, Paso Robles, California

Green lines of topographic art overlook a 20-mile arc of blue ocean to the south. Twenty miles to the north, a castle with Egyptian statuary and

Flemish tapestry stands above a shoreline where a craftswoman finds gems with the look of a full moon and strings them into jewelry. She takes her gems and markets them at a vineyard where two lobes of hill covered in oak, folded in the middle, form a vast evergreen heart set off by rows of grapes.

This place is more kingdom than locale.

At this overlook along Route 46, which many extend into day-use area, morning fog passes like cotton, wetting the vineyards and enabling the acclaimed Fog Catcher wine as it drifts by black sage (*Salvia mellifera*) blossoms that make the kingdom one of honey as well.

Black sage grows along the Pacific's theatre of cliffs and mountainsides where "along the ocean" means "above the ocean". It prefers the view for the abundance of light that the sage botanical family requires. The life-giving light sends black sage growing with abandon in coastal chaparral and oak-studded uplands.

The plant bears a lightness specific to it, blooming in April and May amidst fresh green and setting in motion millions of honeybee wings spending their work days among it. Returning home, they produce a distillation of lightness, a crystal honey. Honey users say that of all the honey works in all the corners of the world, none produces a finer product.

The human body honors this honey with enhanced sugar tolerance. Whereas refined white sugar from cane plantations produces a rapid insulin response through its excess glucose, black sage honey engenders less of a strain through a slower digestion rate and gives our diabetic generation a beneficial alternative. Black sage honey resists crystallization, which gives it a lengthy shelf life that encourages use. Its non-cloying flavor offers further support for regular consumption.

The long shelf life of black sage honey means a long life inside the hive as well. Honeybees sustain themselves with their product during the downtime of the honey production cycle, which in the case of black sage honey, can be as long as two years.

For a traveler who likes to follow organic food to its source, this pull-off along Route 46 educates. Walk to the edge of the line of rocks separating the pull-off from the sloping ranch land to see the plants. If outside of the flowering period, they identify themselves with dark seed heads that lend the plant its name.

For the honey itself, visit Jack Creek Farms, along Route 46 seven miles from Paso Robles. It offers honey tasting, a counterpoint to the wine-tasting experiences offered here. A wide selection of honey varietals provides context.

Honey bears an indirect relation to wine. Though bees do not pollinate grapes, the addition of wildflowers like black sage between the rows draws a host of pollinators that attack insects hostile to grapes. With these twin benefactors of wine and honey, the vineyards of this kingdom restore a singular sense of rightness.

The wine-honey relation represents a holistic joinder of culture and vineyard, a cross-pollination. By necessity, winemakers study the ecology of their land, from climate trends through soil characteristics, with an intensity enabled by modern science. Their knowledge resets the historic landscape and its natural components. Most importantly, the popularity they enjoy means that this fresh knowledge spreads freely.

Visitors to this New Napa find craftswoman and artist Julie Parker at winery trunk shows celebrating the man/earth bond with hand-crafted jewelry sourced from her end of the kingdom, where gems wash up on Moonstone Beach. She obtains her material from semiprecious hoards of red, green and orange pebbles polished by the ocean. The rolling thunder of northwest surf heaps the cosmetic treasure of jade, agate, moonstone, jasper and serpentine, with centuries of ships contributing frosted sea glass fragments. Ms. Parker's work reaches across the waves with her placemats fashioned from recycled wine corks, an ethically re-sourced awareness of the exhaustible cork oak stands in Portugal.

These gem beaches lead the eye toward La Cuesta Encantada, or Hearst Castle. The moon rises behind a castle valued at $5,000,000,000 in current dollars. It literally contains many of the world's finest objects, notable portions of buildings even, culled

from faraway lands, surrounded by 82,000 acres.
Visitors are very much subjects, ferried to the hill on
a bus where they roam the grounds with cameras.

Feel free to gather the gems, the chips of trans-
parent serpentine that look like green sea glass, the
moonstones with their lunar luster and suggestive
roundness answering the rising moon above the castle. The California ideal of simple riches was born
here. The ships drop off their cargo of gems. Julie
Parker sifts through it to the sound of surf, reaching
into the California dream.

PROFILE

Trip Outline: Los Angeles – CA 101-N 97 miles – CA 154-W 34 miles – CA 101-N 57 miles – CA 1-N 10 miles – CA 46-W 5 miles

Difficulty: 0 of 10
Length: 0.01 miles
Elevation Change: 0
Water: No
Toilets: No
Surface: Packed dirt

Best time of year: Either April or October, depending on your color preference. April features bright green views which the dry summer alters to an oak hue.

Along the trail: Your vehicle is with you. Enjoy a snack, pull out portable chairs, assemble your camera tripod or artist's easel. This is a view of consequence, set in a region of change where the enchanting landscape is being responsibly preserved and transformed by the American wine industry.

Hazards: None

CHAPTER 9

Ridgeline

REDWOOD CITY

(*Ohlone Nation*)
Elevation 2200

Skyline Boulevard and Skyline Drive – Pacific
and Atlantic bookends of outdoor America,
they share much. Their latitudes are similar.
Both occupy evergreen ridgelines. Hikers and
mountain bikers fill their roadside parking lots 30
miles from San Francisco and 90 from Washington,
D.C. When done exerting, they have a restaurant
that looks very much like the one where Neil Young
made his Harvest Moon video and the Skyline
Dining Room with blackberry ice cream pie.

Each retains spirits of wilderness. Mountain
lions roam near Skyline Boulevard, essentially spirits
rarely sighted. The timber rattlesnakes of Skyline
Drive appear materially at the tourist overlooks.
The snakes thrive in the tangled abundance of
cleared forest adjacent to stone overlook walls.

"Rattlesnakes like the food and cover that some
overlooks provide," says Shenandoah National Park

biologist Rolf Gubler. "They like rock walls, boulder fields and rock/log access for cover. They also use these areas to bask in the sun. They like the openings of overlooks and scenic vistas because they provide food (small mammals like voles, mice, chipmunks, etc.)."

America's bookends rise into a world of climate change. Along Skyline Drive, warming temperatures aid and abet the destructive hemlock wooly adelgid. This insect strips the eastern hemlock of its needles and has killed nearly all of them there. This however is an ancient ecosystem and this just a turning over of elements. It opens up the scenic views with their transcendent freedom of sunsets and hair-waving wind.

Along Skyline Boulevard at El Corte de Madera Open Space Preserve, the nearby Pacific acts as a great preservative. Its mist feeds the redwood stands with moisture, re-purifying air already cleansed by their dense greenery. The turning of the ecosystem is more deliberate: The Methuselah Redwood at roadside is 1,800 years old. There is an ancient freedom of sensuality here, of red woods of Pacific madrone (*Arbutus menziesii*) and redwood, deep green infusing the air like a painted backdrop.

Paintings and millenia both are insignificant if considered alongside the Pacific, enabler of the redwoods. Any change in the redwoods points to a global, climatic change rather than one of mere weather. When that Pacific system of moisture sends less mist among the redwood trunks, it introduces the broader concept of climate change.

During a 2012-2016 moisture deficit and subsequent death of curated redwoods throughout urban zones of intersections and plazas, there was much conjecture regarding the cause. In the old groves of El Corte de Madera, the conjecture became analysis.

In a recent research initiative, Save The Redwoods League had volunteer citizen scientists monitor the ferns in the redwood understory. The meter-long fronds of sword fern, *Polystichum munitum*, featured on so many calendars, send out new growth each year. During wet years, the frond length is correspondingly greater. Measurements over many years indicate the amount of moisture reaching the base of the ecosystem and indicate overall climate.

Emily Burns, Director of Science at Save The Redwoods, 415-362-2352, summarizes the results of a recent fern study focused on the drought years 2012-14, likely a 1,000-year event. Per her research abstract, "Results showed that *P. munitum* throughout the ecosystem range avoided the drought by reducing total crown leaf area by approximately one-third." This size reduction parallels a latitudinal reduction in moisture from wetter to drier portions of redwood range. Put simply, the ferns retreat under stress and then resurge. This pacing tactic succeeds and hints at similar mechanisms elsewhere in the ecosystem, but it also signals generalized stress.

When climate change affects such a widely regarded part of the American outdoors, it constricts the earth/man relationship. By defeating our efforts to bring the redwoods to our neighborhoods, it puts stress on the fixed supply of land supporting the original stands. The Easterner fleeing dead eastern hemlock branches for the reassuring green of the redwoods senses cross-country change at El Corte de Madera.

Two-foot hemlock saplings along Skyline Drive assure a technical resurgence of the tree but not a cultural one. The pattern of forest succession does not favor a widespread hemlock return, and the annals of the logging industry show a widespread succession of hardwoods for conifers. In these high elevations, sweet birch controls the newly opened understory but will not be able to maintain the cool temperatures that hemlock has — the ever-green, elevated self of earth and its dark chambers of climatic conservatism.

At the apex of the two bookends, red trees parallel each other in the rocky soil — on Skyline Drive, wine-rooted sweet birch; on the slim crest of Skyline Boulevard, pink-trunked Pacific madrone and blood-red manzanita. One particular trail running through El Corte de Madera's 2,906 acres guarantees a meeting with the distinctly western madrone and manzanita.

So many Pacific madrones line the Sierra Morena Trail, the main trail on the west side of the parking area, that a forester might be tempted to name it the Madrone Path. Amateur foresters admire the sunshine touching the bright hues of their trunks.

This tree occupies the redwood/Douglas fir understory here but occasionally achieves dominance. Given a flat niche on the crest, it sheds reddish bark sheathes from branches that rival those of the firs in height in a micro-forest with live oak in the understory.

Manzanita gives Skyline Boulevard cultural separation from Skyline Drive through its blooming time. In the gray depths of January, its leaves drip with rainwater and snow-white blossoms. Contrarian and indomitable, it attains an age measured in centuries.

Its closeness to densely populated San Francisco forces a prohibition on forays off of established trails at El Corte de Madera, making a relationship with this ridgeline a purely aesthetic one. Such a cultural separation — enforced with misdemeanor citations – yields the neutral earth currency exchange of snow-white manzanita blossoms for free range in the Skyline Drive snows.

PROFILE

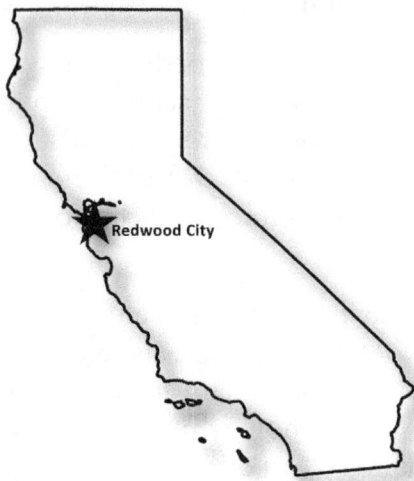

*Trip Outline: San Francisco – CA 101-S 10 miles –
I 380-W 2 miles – I 280-S 9 miles – CA 35-S 12 miles*

Difficulty: 3 of 10
Length: 1.0 miles
Elevation Change: 300
Water: No
Toilets: Yes
Surface: Dirt

*Best time of year: The redwood forest here cools in
summer and shields from winter rains, making this a
walk for all seasons. Arrive early at each of these
Skylines, which are centers for the increased popularity of hiking.*

Along the trail: As the trail descends into the red-woods, the bright yellow Santa Cruz banana slug, a cultural symbol of the region that reaches 10 inches in length, slides across the trail freely in wet weather.

Hazards: Only the occasional poison oak

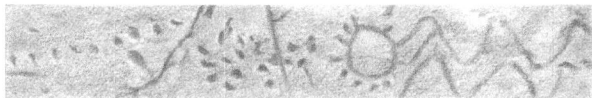

CHAPTER 10

Knoll

LOWER LAKE

(Pomo Nation)
Elevation 2300

The silicon still lies there in the clay 350,000 years after it shot into the air and settled all over the high ground surrounding northern California's volcanic Mount Konocti and 19-mile-long Clear Lake — diamond-like pieces, some mere grains, some nickels. On clear days, here in the least polluted air in California, the diamonds signal like stars from yards away, large and small alike.

All the peoples who have lived here through the centuries have taken note of the Lake County diamonds. The Pomo people placed them on gravesites so that the moon shining on them would frighten away dark spirits. Generations from the pioneers onward have watched for them in plowed fields, then dirt roads, then vineyards. Descendants have worn them as diamonds.

We organize recreational hunts for them today. The quality of the find proves as uncertain as the ancient chronology that yielded it, but they offer relief from souvenir capitalism. Tourists sign up for the Pinzgauer Tour at Six Sigma Vineyard near Lower Lake, which features a 1,700-foot hilltop site where the guide stops for a brief time and passengers dismount so they might see one, touch one, freely select what nature gives.

Technically not diamonds, neither are they mere variations on quartz. They are fragments produced in the pressure of a fierce magma chamber. While they may feature citrine or amethyst tints, those hues, along with an 8.0 hardness suitable for faceting, serve to elevate the differentiation.

They occur on a hilltop-scratching dirt road named Perini Road, where I get down to raw truths. I walk right down the middle of the road. Where the grader has scoured the bed, right there among the grinding tire treadmarks, I see them, their hardness assuring their unscratched wholeness, their superior refracting qualities distinquishing them from glass. The bump of Mount Konocti on the horizon answers the intercepting fist of the knoll.

Though on the topographic hilltop, I am still approaching through dirt to the higher clarity of indigenous peoples time and an earth-born creativity that enfolded the stars and moon and still stands in opposition to cultural destruction. In that time, the lights of stars first came to a sky lit simply by a temperamental sun and gentle moon.

A Pomo chieftain fell in love with the moon and consumed his nights singing to the sky, inciting the selfishness of the sun, who lured him to a high place on Mount Konocti. The moon, spotting the chieftain there, sang beside him, and her words were transmuted into golden dust. The sun encouraged her to return from the mountain and light the seasons for her people, and her tears at parting changed the golden moon-dust into diamonds that fell to earth. The chieftain was left alone.

The sun, seeing the chieftain unaccompanied, attempted to murder him, but the moon fought to save him. She hurled handfuls of golden dust at the sun. Some of the dust stuck in the sky to become stars and some fell as diamonds. The moon then ushered the chieftain into the sky to dwell with her.

The hilltop is quiet, California walnut trees branching soundlessly along the dirt road as I trace a dusty legacy of violence. Mount Konocti stands in the distance beyond rows of grapes. My shoes beat down through the digital, through the industrial, through the agricultural, to ranchers designating the daughters of the moon as sex slaves and men rising up like the sun to murder the persecutors. My shoes beat down through the U.S. Cavalry, who in response boarded boats and surrounded the Pomo on Bloody Island in Clear Lake, impaling infants on gun barrels as their mothers watched and destroying families with artillery.

My shoes stop when I pick up a diamond. I'm a party of one when I find its connecting symbolism –

but not alone. The dirt only 32 miles away, near Upper Lake, holds a stone monument to the Bloody Island Massacre. That dirt marks the genocide of their earth-sky bond, turned into a tomb garnished with Lake County Diamonds.

PROFILE

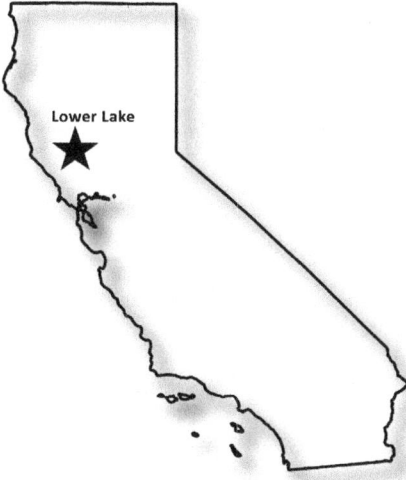

Trip Outline: San Francisco – 101-N 55 miles – CA 29-N 29 miles

Difficulty: 0 of 10
Length: 0.25 miles
Elevation Change: 0
Water: No
Toilets: No
Surface: Dirt

Best time of year: April, after the winter rains and before the summer heat

Along the trail: Scenic vineyards line this dirt road, but the Pinzgauer Tour of the Six Sigma Ranch and

Winery offers an educational and historic vineyard tour as well, including diamond hunting.

Hazards: The occasional car or truck

CHAPTER 11

Peak

FREMONT

(Ohlone Nation)
Elevation 2517

At 8:00 A.M. on a summer Monday morning, dozens of cars fill the parking lot at the hem of Mission Peak on Stanford Avenue in Fremont, as hikers and runners embark on pilgrimages to the golden grasses of its summit. It's an historic and personal backgrounding for the burgeoning East Bay.

Mission Peak takes its name from a venerable Spanish mission, Mission San Jose, that offers a microcosm of California history on its grounds preserved along Fremont Boulevard. A tour of the 1797-era site reveals centuries of events that range from early encounters of priests with local Ohlone people through the mountain's acquisition as a vast rancheria supporting 12,000 cattle through an 1868 earthquake that decimated much of the structure, the salvaged portion of which retains its huge wooden beams.

The tourist brochures reveal nothing about the stone walls. On the crest of Mission Peak, as well as 50 miles of similar California Coast Range ridgelines, ancient stone walls of undetermined origin run. Each hiker forms a personal opinion regarding who constructed them. The privilege of speculation on the walls comes only after a 3-mile climb of over 2,000 vertical feet that takes at least 2 hours up a well-kept and heavily used trail. The parking lot area features a water fountain offering a final chance to fill bottles for the arid and wind-swept trek. Go in the morning to mitigate the relentless sun, and bring a wide-brimmed hat.

The trail presses an old roadbed into service for much of its length as it climbs past iconic live oaks and yellow poppies as distinctive western wildlife ranges about. I saw my first coyote on Mission Peak in this open landscape where ground squirrels scurry and the sky-colored Western bluebird launches from the brush.

The Mission Peak trail crest joins with the developing Bay Area Ridge Trail, a footpath that will ultimately stretch 500 miles and connect 75 public parks and open space preserves. The East Bay Regional Park District now encompasses over 90,000 acres of greenbelt parkland serving its 7,000,000 residents.

From the summit, a panorama of significant geography opens up: the blue San Francisco Bay below, San Francisco itself to the northwest, the

Santa Cruz Mountains walling off the Pacific view; and to the east under ideal conditions, the snowy peaks of the Sierra Nevada.

Here runs one of those mysterious stone walls, the bay below and the entire continent at its back, suggesting some large-scale geographic statement. The likely suspects offer no indication of involvement, with nothing in Spanish records or Native American tradition. Speculation extends as far as an ancient Chinese landing on our shores and subsequent colonization, but the waving grasses and warm, lichen-blotched stones offer as confirmation only a faint hint of something personally and historically meaningful.

Human beings have a long and broad spectrum of interactions with high ground. Maybe the walls are an accretion of actions spurred by the huge stones scattered far above. Maybe the edge of a native prayer circle became a pioneer property boundary, or ranchers wanting to prevent their stock from eluding their line of sight over the ridgetops added stones to those arrayed by prehistoric people.

These provocative walls overlooking the Berkeley-Oakland-Fremont side of San Francisco play a contemporary ecological role more tangible than their widely speculated cultural one. They have become an element of the land from which they were gathered up. Their demarcating structure supports a natural culture.

They trap moisture and soil, encouraging the growth of native shrubs and wildflowers that build a sheltering habitat similar to that created by English fencerows. Insects frequent the flowers, birds such as the Western meadowlark (*Sturnella neglecta*) consume the insects, ground squirrels forage for plant seeds. The linear preserve extends into the air, where golden eagles sail by in search of ground squirrels, Pacific rattlesnakes (*Crotalus oreganus*) and California slender salamanders (*Batrachoseps attenuatus*).

At night, bobcats, gray foxes and occasional cougars follow the lines of the walls in search of small birds, on the heels of a long-lost community of human builders. On these embellished ridgetops, flora and fauna align themselves in a link to an unknown past.

PROFILE

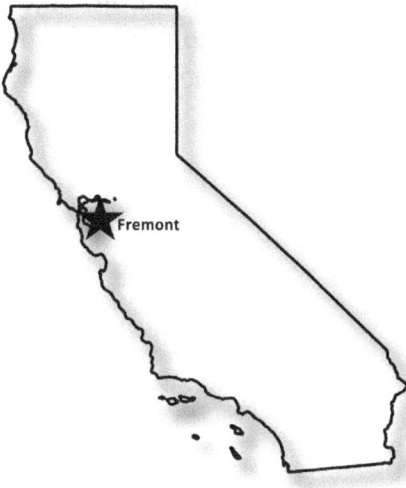

Trip Outline: San Francisco – 101-S 37 miles; CA 84-E 10 miles

Difficulty: 10 of 10
Length: 5 miles
Elevation Change: 2000
Water: Yes
Toilets: Yes
Surface: Dirt

Best time of year: April, when the ground has dried but the heat has yet to set in

Along the trail: Inspiring views of the East Bay and excellent wildlife and bird viewing

Hazards: Remember that these vast grasslands retain their standing as wilderness despite the millions of people below. In 2017, a hiker suffered a rattlesnake bite at the summit of the trail. In summer, dehydration becomes a concern. Beware of poison oak.

CHAPTER 12

Razorback Bench

JOLON

(Salinan Nation)
Elevation 3000

Coulter pines (*Pinus coulteri*) are a conifer species restricted almost exclusively to California; and like many things Californian, they come with an exclamation point. Their cones are the largest in the world, with a miniature tree shape and weight that can exceed 10 pounds, woods lore warnings for unschooled campers setting up beneath the boughs they drop from.

In a state with over 60 species of conifers where gathering those of the abundant ponderosa and out-sized sugar are picnic customs, Coulter pine habitat is unexpected. Climbing up Nacimiento-Fergusson Road from the backside of Fort Hunter-Liggett, through 20 twisting miles above a canyon where mountain lions range, the ascent gives out at two pine-needled parking spaces 3,000 feet above the ocean. Beneath a pair of trees, outlandish pine cones lie among vacation-spoiling poison oak.

At this high crossroads where acorn woodpeckers ply the live oak branches that drink the ocean fog, a hybrid trail/dirt road overseen by Coulter pines climbs to Cone Peak, America's alpha ocean view at around 5,000 feet. The Pacific breathes eastward here, balancing tree growth limits that the shallow soil presents in a relationship that climate change periodically adjusts. Drought episodes such as that in 2012-2016 compromise their immunity to deadly beetle infestation, but atmospheric rivers of rain flow directly over the exposed ridgeline, sprouting trees and ensuring that the splendid cones hit the ground each year and roll.

This line of dirt, the Coast Ridge Trail, traverses the ridgeline with inspiring simplicity. The exposed surface provides a safe zone from the occasional rattlesnake in the grass as well as unsullied views fashioned of fresh air, ocean and amber hills. The Trail runs for a total of 22 miles between Cone Peak and Los Burros Road.

The ecology of Coulter pine is an exclamation point within an exclamation point. Gathering a cone from some precipitous slope brings a kind of reverse recognition. The exclamation point of California wildfires opening the cones and releasing the seeds faces the exclamation point of mudslides like the one that followed a 16-inch rainfall near the two parking spaces under the pines.

Holding a Coulter pine cone, my reverse recognition materializes in a potential cougar encounter.

Below these trees, the land pitches at a treacherous rate into a rocky canyon encompassed by hundreds of thousands of untouched acres. It's the most rugged ground I have ever seen in the United States and likely den of the cougar recently sighted on Hunter-Liggett. Enter defensively, with the intimidating presence of companions and a noisy sidearm.

Millions of people have grown up without mountaintops, not even knowing what a pine cone looks like. Those who gather them become California ambassadors and semi-entrepreneurs with an online exclamation point of $50 per cone. A mountain and ocean recognition materializes for the concrete-bound as they look at their Christmas-tree-shaped cones, trimmed to stand upright, varnished, graced with painted live oak acorns.

PROFILE

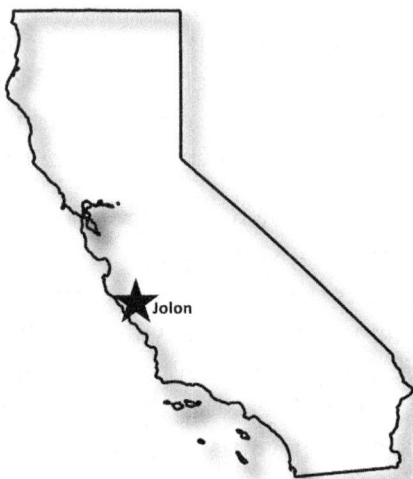

*Trip Outline: San Francisco – 101-S 11 miles – I
280-S 24 miles —   CA 85-S 19 miles – 101-S 113
miles— Jolon Road 26 miles — Fort Hunter-Liggett
gate – sign for Route 1 – green bridge — left at crossroads with Nacimiento-Fergusson signage.   Check
with Los Padres National Forest for weather-related
road closures. Nacimiento-Fergusson road is closed
until December 2023 due to severe fire/mudslide
damage.*

*Difficulty: 0 of 10
Length: 1 mile
Elevation Change: 0
Water: No
Toilets: No
Surface: Dirt*

Best time of year: May, after the winter dangers of road washouts and landslides

Along the trail: A pure spectacle of untouched Pacific Ocean views

Hazards: A dirt road appropriated as a trail with the only hazard the rare vehicle. The occasional rattlesnake and ubiquitous poison oak await steps taken off of the trail. The deer population attracts cougars.

CHAPTER 13

Desert Inselberg

TWENTY-NINE PALMS

(Chemahuevi Nation)
Elevation 3800

Driving in the dark through San Bernardino, past Coachella, then beyond to Joshua Tree National Park, I began wandering around, jumping from one rock to another until I sat down, perching in a pile of rock rubble at 7:30 A.M. on April 11, 2014.

I had entered by parking at the first trail lot on the left side of the main road through the park, about 2 miles in from the west entrance. My trail, the North Canyon Trail, ran for 1.2 miles, but I stepped off of it and scrambled up to a vantage point on a desolate terrace in the morning coolness. My perch above the canyon was essentially an eroding mountain formed of a rock known as monzogranite.

Throughout Joshua Tree, there is a differential process of erosion, creating topographic relief and the summary geologic rock pile framing the temporal habitation I had found.   Particular rock piles with pronounced definition are called inselbergs. The disarray of Joshua Tree inselbergs is aptly invoked through the word "sledgehammer".

Rocks and wildflowers complete for popularity among the nearly 1.5 million visitors to Joshua Tree's 800,000 acres. In the 1930s, prior to its 1936 designation as a National Monument and eventual 1994 christening as a National Park, officials suggested the name Desert Plants National Park. Today, this expanse attracts rock climbers from all over the world who consider it a premier year-round destination.

The early hour and long drive receded from my mind, and the silence granted me visual focus. An apricot-orange wildflower materialized a few yards ahead of me. Its structural perfection and arresting vividness exceeded hundreds of species I knew from both coasts and 20 or more new ones I saw there in the early morning light blooming in this vast rubble pile. These defining lines of beauty were a desert mariposa lily (*Calachortus kennedyi*).

Evidently, April 11, 2014 and Joshua Tree were the coordinates for the ideal American desert experience. It wasn't just the desert mariposa lily.   In three hours of drifting over a mere several hundred yards of terrain, I saw two species of expansive-flowered pink cactus, the hedgehog (*Echinocereus engelmannii*) and beavertail (*Opuntia basilaris var. basilaris*), as well as the waxy yellow barrel cactus

(*Ferocactus cylindranceus*). Vari-colored wildflowers, multiple species per frame, invited photographs
in the clear light. Occasionally, one called desert
dandelion (*Malacothrix glabrata*) actually carpeted
the ground.

This rock rubble pile of many miles is a repository
of life. Wildflower seeds lie intact for long periods,
undisturbed among countless crevices and odd
angles of shadow. Cactus wrens (*Campylorhynchus
brunneicapillus*) burst into song at dawn. Black-
crested flycatchers (*Phainopepla nitens*) perch on
scrubby oak trees. The Joshua trees (*Yucca brevifolia*)
themselves have grown unmolested for 700 or more
years. This is a rock pile but a pristine rock pile,
never farmed, never logged, basically unaltered.

My timing was perfect not only to the day but to
the hour. I returned to the car in the strengthening
sunlight and admired a beavertail cactus blossom,
then glanced up into the view of a snow-capped
mountain through a Joshua tree branch. The roadside was filling up with cars as visitors followed me
in celebration of Desert Spring.

In the unpleasant heat, I saw a browning cholla
cactus, a reminder of how temperatures are bringing
to Joshua Tree a distinctive desolation that worsens
each year. Climate change is transforming a landscape threatening for waterless hikers into one that
bakes away its own vegetation. To view this change
firsthand, witnesses need only enter where I did, 50
miles from Palm Springs, average July day. The park

road ascends gradually beyond the visitor center, attaining a cooler plateau studded with photogenic rock formations.

What look like giant green paintbrushes stand among the high ground rocks – the saplings of Joshua trees. In an exodus from the overheated flats, the species has seeded itself at the higher elevation, taking with it the yucca moths (*Tegeticula yuccasella*) that pollinate it, together with the rest of its ecological subsystem of plants and animals. The pollinating moths occupy the ground at its base as well as the tree blossoms.

Joshua Trees

Dr. Cameron W. Barrows, ecologist at the University of California-Riverside, discovered the Joshua tree migration. He currently analyzes the many lower profile relationships among life forms among life forms in the park to determine how climate change is stressing those bonds. In 2016, he inaugurated a study on 45 species of mammals, birds, plants, reptiles, and amphibians, ranking each according to its projected vulnerability to climate change. Researchers will apportion a segment of Joshua Tree landscape and monitor the presence of these lifeforms over a period of years. They intend to enlist the aid of citizen-scientists in order to facilitate the laborious and time-consuming legwork that the project requires.

The road leading uphill from the Oasis Visitor Center follows a transition zone between two ecological regions, enhancing both the visibility and impact of climate change. Global warming is readjusting life within the transition zone. The fiercely hot Sonoran Desert at the visitor center sends its emblematic cholla cactus into the Mojave Desert several miles up the mountainside, in evident pursuit of the fleeing Joshua trees. This makes for an intriguing study environment for Dr. Barrows and colleagues.

A second lifeform that desert visitors regard as emblematic is also undergoing climate change adjustment. The chuckwalla lizard (*Sauromalus ater*), sunning on the rocks like a miniature dinosaur, reaching 18 inches in length, subsists on vegetation. Drought patterns that reduce the abundance of plants place stress on the fearsome-appearing but harmless lizard.

Climate change here is a revolution involving death through heat and dryness, but it amounts to a redrawing of boundaries rather than a disaster. The average person views the flight of the Joshua trees and sees the Sonoran Desert overtaking the Mojave Desert. Dr. Barrows cautions that the entirety of a region is more than the existence of a single plant. Ecology is a science that studies patterns while admitting the limits of its statistics.

"The boundaries of what we now call the Mojave Desert, climatically and biologically, will shift as a result of modern climate change. That will probably mean shifts to higher elevations and perhaps further north and west. That could mean a contraction or an expansion. The complexities of what constrain and enable movements/shifts of ecoregions, such as the Mojave Desert, exceed our current understandings."

Lifted by Desert Spring, Californians from Coachella to Joshua Tree celebrate, while each year, the organic emblems of nature and their human counterparts move a bit further up into the rocks, smiling faces darkened by centuries of sun, advancing into pale and precarious footholds.

PROFILE

Trip Outline: Los Angeles – I-10 100 miles – CA 62 43 miles

Difficulty: 3 of 10
Length: 5 miles
Elevation Change: 600
Water: No
Toilets: No
Surface: Dirt/sand

Best time of year: April, when temperature is reasonably cool and the wildflowers are blooming. Contact the park at 760-367-5502 to inquire about the progress of flower blooms.

Along the trail: A rich variety of birds and flowers,

together with the park's namesake Joshua trees, grace this basically flat trail.

Hazards: Rattlesnakes and heat. By no means wander off of the trail in the heat of summer. Under those conditions, the park is a proven killer.

CHAPTER 14

Elevated Meadow

EL PORTAL

(*Ahwahnechee Nation*)
Elevation 4000

*T*he visitor absorbing the vast picnic-like meadow of Yosemite amid the finest pine/fir forest on earth sees the spectre of a dead pine tree as an assault. Tall and brown, it foregrounds the audible vista of 2,245-foot Yosemite Falls while 617-foot Bridal Veil Falls plunges behind the vantage point. I noted the dead tree there in 2014.

Pines desecrated in the inner sanctum of our nation's favorite park: what is the nature of such a brazen intrusion? What is its identity? We hear of bark beetles, episodic drought, climate change. Beetles and drought killed this tall pine, but they represent the short tree of technical thought, events within a larger context. Look to the forest, the tall thought of climate change.

When we talk about climate, we talk about something fixed and indeterminate; a condition or state, if you will. This is as opposed to weather, which consists of events. Definitional thinking places climate as the enabler of weather and of natural occurrences such as drought and bark beetles.

Illustration: Julie Parker, Paso Robles, California

By definition, climate implies a lengthy time period. This ponderosa pine (*Pinus ponderosa*), as a species, has 300-500 years of potential life. Were they transplants from nurseries, we could assign blame for their demise to weather or insects attacking a vulnerable tree in a new environment, but it takes hundreds of years of corresponding destructive force to produce such a result in the heart of ponderosa country, amidst trees with centuries-long lifespans.

The ponderosa is the bellwether conifer species of California. In pure Christmas-like stands, it flanks hundreds of miles of highways from the slopes of Shasta to Big Bear, but most notably in the northern part of the state where grassy manzanita and oak yield to conifers as the elevation increases. When the horrific Camp Fire ignited on a grassy power line above the Feather River in 2018, it found vast stands of ponderosa to feed upon as it overtook the town of Paradise, population 25,000, and destroyed it, killing 88 people.

The destructive force cutting into centuries-old lifespans is rising forest temperature. The earth warms and combusts more readily, particularly when carpeted with pine straw. The same conditions that induced Yosemite's 2013 Rim Fire – increased heat, baking vegetation – draw bark beetles, which brown the ponderosas of Yosemite.

The off-color pine in the foreground of the vista I viewed in 2014 was not an isolated pine death. Entire mountain slopes in the surrounding Sierra stand brown, with the destructive force no respecter of species. Both ponderosa and sugar pines – another long-lived species – are victimized. The orientation; or as foresters say, "aspect," of this spectacle points to its climatic genesis. These slopes orient south and west, toward the searing Mojave Desert and the furnace-like Central Valley.

Scientists lack instruments capable of ascertaining conditions 500 years ago, leaving reasoning and instinct sharpened by immersive hikes in these forests to uncover old processes. Well-defined tree zones corresponding to elevation levels aid the interpretation. John Muir in the classic *The Mountains of California* expounds on conifer zones and provides the overview of the forces behind landscapes and their relation to each other here, embedded within splendid paragraphs of nature appreciation.

In this instance, respect for his hikes and observations, which combine natural history and spirituality, leads to the truth more readily than redundant data clutter of researchers. A basic walk through the zonal bands of forest here exposes chronological processes and validates the principle of climate change. It demonstrates that oak trees are supplanting, rather than succeeding, conifers, which is not natural given that science tells us that centuries-old conifers constitute the climax forest. Simply look for pine stumps beneath oaks to see the elevation shift in zones. Change is underfoot.

Nothing prevents visitors from simply parking and strolling through the grasses in this sitting room of Yosemite's mansion, but the park accommodates hikers with the popular 2-mile Sentinel Meadow/ Cook's Meadow Loop. A true Trail of the People, its flat surface crosses two rustic bridges, offers rest spots, and presents the classic view of the Merced River with towering Yosemite Falls crowning it far up the river valley.

The brown ponderosas blight the tourist experience, which is why workers cast their sawn woodchunks, along with fragrant incense cedar, in a shadowed side-lot near Yosemite Falls. We come here to see the permanence and stability of the earth, when the truth is that climate change itself is a mere event within a matrix of eons and that larger forces in the tall trees of thought govern the park's very existence.

PROFILE

*Trip Outline: San Francisco – I 580-E 68 miles —
CA-62 43 miles*

*Difficulty: 0 of 10
Length: 2 miles
Elevation Change: 0
Water: Yes
Toilets: Yes
Surface: Dirt*

*Best time of year: April, when the apple blossoms left
over from pioneer habitation foreground Yosemite
Falls at peak flow*

*Along the trail: This hike has a social quality, with
visitors from all over the world enjoying it. Because*

it combines river, mountain and forest scenery, millions of photographs originate here.

Hazards: None

CHAPTER 15

Volcanic Tableland

TULE LAKE

(*Modoc Nation*)
Elevation 4400

Geology is like a slow war.

– Stephanie Schneider, Park Ranger,
Lava Beds National Monument

*L*ava Beds National Monument is more planetary than national. The lunar-white overlord
of Shasta floats at 14,000 feet above a battlefield where one race of human being sought to
extinguish another. The landscape is a Hell of 110-
degree heat and jagged lava ripped apart in fissures.
Pictographs speak from a wall lit by the orange
California sunset.

Volcanism laid the battlefield floor. Roughly
30,000 years ago, nearby Schonchin Butte erupted,
releasing a lava flow, the Schonchin Flow, that
killed everything in its path and left behind terra

cotta-toned rocks with air holes inhabited by spiders. One thousand years ago, grains of white pumice poured down from an eruption of neighboring Glass Mountain, affording the combatants in the Modoc War crunchy battle footing more secure than that of sharp lava.

At least 30 discrete volcanic events created layered beds of lava riddled with caves and crevices, home to bats, swallows, ravens and the native warriors who disappeared within the earth as subterranean soldiers. The Modoc utilized this geology to render themselves invincible for five months in the Modoc War of 1872, achieving a 53-15 casualty differential despite a 1000-50 combatant deficit.

One night, their water supply cut off, the Modoc shepherded their women and children beneath the undulating landscape of western juniper and mountain mahogany comprising the 47,000 acres of Lava Beds. Bubbling gases formed small caves that sheltered them. Partial tunnels of lava called "surface tubes" saved them from capture.

One June day many years ago, I began hiking Lava Beds at the Indian Wells campground, across from the NPS Visitor Center, amythest carpet phlox blanketing the cave-pocked landscape that evacuated the combatants in the face of Army mortar fire that drove them from their stronghold directly to the north.

The trail system leads past Skull Cave, a cold subterranean site 110 feet deep. Ice coats the bottom-most reaches of Skull Cave, named for the remains of animals as well as humans discovered within during the 19th century. The bighorn sheep and mountain goats that once inhabited this grassy high desert contributed their remains to the lava beds, as well as the Modoc cattle that supplanted them and spared the warriors and their families from starvation.

At the southern edge of Modoc war headquarters, Captain Jack's Stronghold, natural basalt walls enclosed a plateau that formed a cattle corral for the tribe and also afforded an escape route when the war turned against them. In silence and under cover of darkness on April 16, 1873, 150 people slipped over a narrow corridor of the Schonchin Flow that led them beyond the cattle corral on an asphalt-black highway of sorts. Centuries of living outdoors taught them the locations of secure footfalls.

My 10-mile trek followed terrain about 2 miles east of the main battlefield on the Three Sisters Loop, named for a congregation of cinder cones formed from volcanic eruptions. As I lunched beneath tree branches, the three stood there behind me – spectral sisters, scorched black.

The crisp pumice turned sharply north, abutting the National Monument boundary, and passed through an historic stand of Western juniper (*Juniperus occidentalis*). The ground undulations created by their massive roots, and their habit of sprouting new growth from weathered branches, suggested great age. The unbroken blanket of pumice nestled against the upwelling roots evidenced that the volcanic matter descended on them 900 years ago.

The trail continues within an historic dialogue of fire. In 2016, another species of flame raced over Lava Beds from a lightning-struck wildfire, the Caldwell Fire. Opportunistic NPS archaeologist David Curtis led a two-year inventory of the compromised battlefield, which revealed itself in bullets, howitzer fragments, rock bulwarks – a re-set of destruction.

Lava Beds functioned as a harsh refuge for both the Modocs and the birds and animals they knew. Birds and animals love complex terrain. Rocky hiding places mean 217 species of birds frequent the Monument, along with animals such as bobcats, packrats and spotted skunks, all attracted to the network of secret places.

In this Earth College major of Desert Life, the unidentified creatures of 80-mph desert drives roam about within walking distance of each other and of the visitors unfamiliar with them. Climate-controlled with classic desert heat, sanitized with classic sagebrush fragrance, it carries a passing grade of Survival.

PROFILE

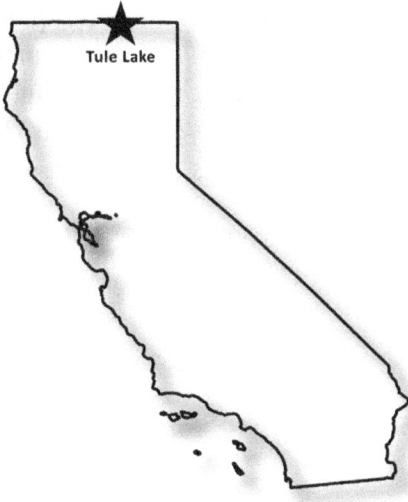

*Trip Outline: San Francisco – I 80-E 55 miles – I
505-N 34 miles – I 5-N 126 miles — CA 299-E 89
miles — Bieber Lookout Road 31 miles — CA 139-
N 11 miles — Rd. 44 N 01 13 miles*

Difficulty: 10 of 10
Length: 10 miles
Elevation Change: 0
Water: No
Toilets: No
Surface: Dirt/pumice
Best time of year: Spring

*Along the trail: The NPS Visitor Center is a comfort-
ing and helpful presence amidst a remote area.*

Hazards: Devote a full day to the Three Sisters Loop in order to conserve energy and absorb the sense of place in this unusual environment. Carry adequate food and water, particularly in the heat of summer; and if for no other reason than that this park is lightly visited. It is common to see no-one in your 10 miles. Beware the usual rattlesnakes and poison oak.

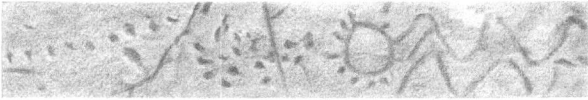

CHAPTER 16

Terrace

PEARBLOSSOM

(*Kitanemuk Nation*)
Elevation 4740

A t 1,310-acre Devil's Punchbowl, in Angeles National Forest, casual visitors witness plants with lifespans of up to 1,000 years dying. Brown color supplants green along the park entrance road. They see it at the parking lot and at trailside in this unique setting at an interface of the San Gabriel Mountains and Mojave Desert.

"There used to be junipers all over there," says David Numer of the entrance road flora. Numer, superintendent of Devil's Punchbowl, has observed the local flora for 42 years and cites a "15-20-year" dry period causing plant migration upslope into cooler sections of the park away from accessible potions. The Punchbowl is located at 4,740 feet.

This is one of the most accommodating of parks for tourists curious about climate change. Numer points to a tree trunk cross-section at the nature center there. Thin rings indicate dry years, wide rings wet years. This is formal Exhibit A of climate change, but informal exhibits abound.

The land rises into a flat bench and parking lot, where a dead pinyon pine (*Pinus monophylla*) appears in countless tourist photos. David explains that bark beetles caused this death but that climate change brought the bark beetles. Excessive heat causes a reduction in pine sap levels. Bark beetles no longer become trapped in the sticky sap and prey unimpeded on the tree. "Bark beetles actually eat the cambium layer of the tree. On dead pinyon pines, you find beetles, but not the bark beetles, which have already moved to the next tree."

The Punchbowl itself is a testament to geologic force. Three hundred feet deep, it formed when the combined influence of the San Andreas, Punchbowl and Pinyon earthquake faults tilted layers of sedimentary rock into picturesque forms. To this day, the Mojave Desert is sliding past the base of the San Gabriel Mountains here at a rate of 2 inches annually, creating constant subterranean tensions.

One look near the head of the trail into the bowl, a 1.1-mile loop, reveals the force of climate change. Here, the manzanita that inhabits the hybrid desert/mountain zone has turned brown.

Change here results in a faunal migration inverse to that of the floral flight upward. Bighorn sheep and mule deer abandon surrounding high country springs as they dry up. They resort to the relatively lower elevation of park acreage. Since water flows downhill, springs at higher elevations disappear first. The water, upon reaching the gentler angle of slope here, spreads outward, developing a life-sustaining aquifer. This hydrologic refuge now allows unusual views of wildlife attracted to browse plants supported by the aquifer. "We see bighorn sheep at Devil's Chair," a popular vista in the park, notes Numer.

This elevational response to heat and dryness, the flight to moisture zones, leads to potential species decimation. What happens when the junipers and pinyon pines migrate into bare rock? Paralleling human lives since our beginnings, Devil's Punchbowl hosts changes in each against its spectacle of stone.

The dead pinyon pine and fleeing manzanitas foreground a geologic vista reflecting change greater than climate change. Bearing in mind Numer's observation that " the Mojave Desert was once a wetland " brings a comforting perspective, considering that in September 2020, the inevitable fire, the Bobcat Fire, consumed heat-stressed Devil's Punchbowl, destroying the nature center, presenting informal Exhibit A.

PROFILE

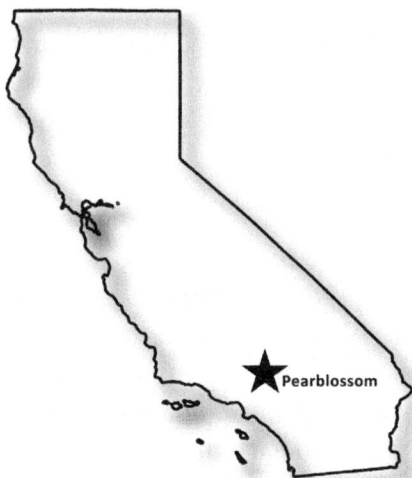

Trip Outline: Los Angeles – 101-N 10 miles – CA 170-N 6 miles — I 5-N 9 miles — CA 14-N 29 miles — Sierra Hwy 5 miles — CA 138-E 8 miles

Difficulty: 4 of 10
Length: 1.1 miles
Elevation Change: 300
Water: Yes
Toilets: Yes
Surface: Dirt
Best time of year: October

Along the trail: Though the loop trail beginning at the visitor center and descending into the Punchbowl has undergone signage restoration, the visitor center itself sustained great damage during the Bobcat Fire.

Nevertheless, the parking lot is ample and the trail located conveniently close to it. The Punchbowl is a prime example of ecological change resulting from desert encroaching on mountain ground as a result of a warming climate.

CHAPTER 17

Escarpment

CEDARVILLE

(*Paiute Nation*)
Elevation 5750

*T*he Warner Escarpment is high desert on a pedestal. Rather than ascending gradually from the hot valley of sagebrush on the California/Nevada border, the country abruptly leaps. The pedestal, built of basalt, rises above the gleam of the alkaline valley as the morning sun strikes its face in the pure and cool air. Structurally, it is a near-vertical façade left in place when the earth alongside it collapsed thousands of feet down to form the dividing valley. It is linear high ground, sharp-sided, with a precipitous scenic view accompanying its 85-mile length. Lacking forest cover, it offers an open garden moistened by winter snows.

The escarpment balances a garden of superbly drained soil studded with wildflower gems. The ground is as soft as powdered cocoa. The elements of the gems intermingle: orange indian paintbrush with gold wooly mule's ears (*Wyethia mollis*), sierra onion (*Allium campanulatum*), with blue lupine (*Lupinus latifolius*). From the east comes a morning flood of desert light that combines with the elevation of the soil to produce a defined wildflower community.

The high garden elevates desert plant life into the presence of an overseeing garden plant, a plateau-filtered higher form. A mountain mahogany tree (*Cercocarpus ledifolius*) perches there on the edge of the structure, rock and air beneath it, catching the dry sun. It curls and spreads, celebrating its freedom from the dusty, root-filled flats of the sagebrush ranches below.

The Paiute tribe esteemed mountain mahogany for its health-sustaining virtues, perhaps acknowledging its ability to eke out 1,000 years of living on the rock and thin soil. The Mexicans call their mountain mahogany "wise tree", *arbol de la sabiduria*, for its longevity and ability to colonize untenable footholds above precipices such as this one – as a friend from that country says, living a long life in a stationary position, without exertion, through perfect adaptation to light and heat.

The mountain mahogany, together with the elemental ponderosa pine, are among the few trees standing on the Warner Plateau. The latter achieves, even with diminished dimensions brought about by the trying environment, aesthetics of dappled orange bark, stout straightness and golden cones.

What remains standing of the Warner Mountains casts a rain shadow to the west that keeps the escarpment bereft of trees, which allows wildflowers to respond to the intense light of midsummer and bloom in great variety. The flat desert to the east forecloses any spread of forest onto the escarpment from that direction. The open façade of the escarpment is subject to erosion, further limiting the prospects for tree growth.

The escarpment, as a structure, is not uniform, but features many angles that either accept or reject the direct sun at a given time of day, unlike the flat valley lying under its direct rays from dawn until dusk. Wildflowers demand these angles and will not tolerate unrelenting sunlight in most cases, nor the constant heat of a featureless plain. It is light that supports these flowers, angles of light and their modifying effect on heat.

The pedestal cracks at Cedar Pass, rock walls shooting up on both sides, while, at the base, wild roses grace the stones where the Paiute tribe walked annually into their high-country summer home. The route was an unchanging one transacted with the inner earth, rock enclosing it. Its deep coolness foreshadowed the coolness of their high country and its pink wild roses.

As the Paiutes walked through the crack in the escarpment, the wildflowers accompanied them with a delicacy replicated in the clean meadows. The flowers they saw are the flowers we see, because time brings no alteration to rock as it would to timbered earth. The morning coolness allows the fragile blue baby blue-eyes (*Nemophila menziesii*) along this wayside to thrive just as the high country coolness fosters the alpine species.

Some of the flowers here are the flowers of the dry roadlessness fronting empty Nevada, while others reflect the increased elevation. Cushion buckwheat (*Eriogonum ovalifolium*), lemon-yellow, spreads here, with white dusty maiden (*Chaenactic douglasii*). Balloon pod milk-vetch (*Astragalus whitneyi*) opens on the uncluttered table of earth.

For several mornings in a row, I awakened near the Nevada border and, my driving hands chilly in the yet-shaded canyon, traveled west to the Paiutes' pass, following the original First Nations path at creekside and then ascending the east wall of it over disused ranchland to the escarpment crest. There in the midst of the searing heat of the July days, wildflowers of all colors spread out over the landscape, wildflowers of so many kinds that I expected a new species with every few steps of elevation gained.

Near 6,000 feet, Oregon sunshine (*Eriophyllum lanatum*) finds here the coolness of more northerly places for its flecks of bright yellow, and penstemon and phloxes decorate footfalls. The penstemon offers the blue sky: *Penstemon humilis* in dusk-blue. These mornings find the phlox species *Ph. Hoodii* carpeting the ground with white alongside a juniper shrub.

Here, an entire mountain chain dropped into emptiness, leaving blankness as commemoration, save for wildflower names themselves reflective of linguistic blankness. With no European botanists wandering around in wool coats to lend them their names, some took the identity of the animals consuming or huddling beneath them. There is the luminous lavender of coyote mint (*Monardella villosa*). Jade-colored rabbit brush (*Chrysothamnus*) shelters coyote mint blossoms.

These wildflowers are a seeding of the pure simplicity of air through which the earth fell, memorials to a cataclysm that no-one witnessed.

PROFILE

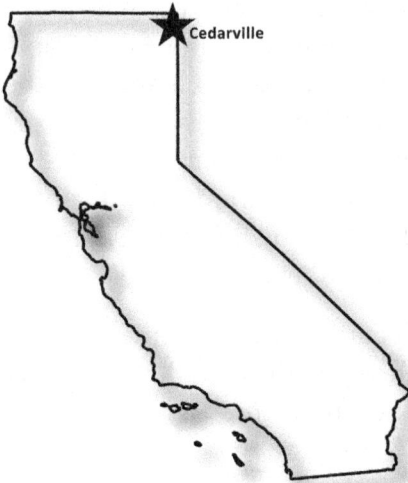

Trip Outline: San Francisco — I 80-E 29 miles — Exit 30B toward Sacramento 10 miles — I 80-E toward Sacramento 15 miles — I 505-N 34 miles — I 5-N 126 miles — CA 299-E 100 miles – CA 139-N 46 miles — CA 299-E 17 miles

Difficulty: 4 of 10
Length: 6 miles
Elevation Change: 790
Water: No
Toilets: No
Surface: Dirt

Best time of year: July, the peak season for wildflowers. Phone 530-233-5811 for information on the progression of wildflower season.

Along the trail: The trail features a kiosk with a nicely produced trail pamphlet free for the taking and ends at a mountaintop ski area.

Hazards: Rattlesnakes and poison oak

CHAPTER 18

Granite Dome

THREE RIVERS

(*Mono Nation*)
Elevation 6460

The road to the crowning path winds uphill in hairpin curves for over 15 miles – over 6,000 vertical feet – before the suite of definitive Sequoia National Park trees appears, set in solid rock at the crest of a granite cliff, a hiking path fronting them in the mountain sun.

A few steps back amidst the conifers, a specimen of the largest tree on earth stands laughing in the shadows. No other tree matches giant sequoia (*Sequoia gigantea*) in size. The dimensional achievement of the great entity reflects the miles of great ascending wildness, rock-studded and diverse.

The ascent maintains a dialogue between rock and tree. Chalky-white California sycamore trees (*Platanus racemosa*) frame a view of towering cliffs the pale tone of their peeled bark. Mountain mahogany shimmers in the sun as if inhabiting an eternal spring.

Along the crowning trail, the Beetle Rock Trail, the lesser players in the forest shrink to reduced size in the demanding conditions, while the sequoia retains its gigantic dimensions. The others become miniatures on the infertile rock surface that forms the trail, striving for endurance in the stony holds, but as befits a tree that has found immortality, it stands broad and straight as a vertical house.

Its reflection of indestructible cheer reaches even the valley floor far below. Rather than nondescript apple or peach orchards, there are sun-drenched flats brightened by golden lemons and oranges. The high country snow waters them with a rushing river that flows fresh even after months of rainless blue skies.

To uplift us with sunset-colored columns and give us pause with their form and longevity – this is their role when we step into their forest. First Nations felt those sentiments, as well as Europeans for nearly two of the 20 centuries that their trunks have outlasted the fall of ancient Rome and travels of Columbus.

They can live for 3,000 years or more.

If America had an arboreal symbol, it would be the sequoia, superior in earthly size, thriving in the most trying environments. Boasting built-in adaptations to the fires at the front lines of the climate crisis, neither will it relinquish its role as conifer region gatekeeper easily. Between 2020 and 2021, wildfires mounted two assaults on the Sequoia Nation's estimated 80,000 citizens. The first took out 10 %, the next 5%.

The fires will be back. Lesser species such as ponderosa pine, dead from bark beetles, have aggravated the intensity of the flames blown to the feet of the giant trees, but they can't burn rock. The sequoia on the ledge at Beetle Rock overlooks all of the turmoil unscathed.

The 0.5 miles to Beetle Rock from Giant Forest Museum is a walk inside a spectacle. Technicalities of botany and geology mean little when the trail is a towering chamber and then a great window pane upon an entire region of California. The asphalt surface and handicapped access affirm the path's status in the hiking community.

The longevity of these trees amplifies their influence beyond basic forest ecology, possibly playing into larger climatic effects as a kind of botanical element. They mark a boundary between the dessicated ridges of southern California and forested Sierra to the north, and their fire resistance helps maintain that boundary, fostering a permanent ecological scheme.

Culturally, they have lifted up the human race for thousands of years. Science admits that their deaths come from simply toppling over rather than through any known disease. Maybe they are a statement from a human past of Biblical figures achieving hundreds-year-old lifespans. Maybe they are truly originals, inspiring us to live peacefully in high places.

PROFILE

Trip Outline: Los Angeles — 101-N 10 miles – CA 170-N 6 miles — I 5-N 67 miles — CA 99-N 31 miles — CA 65-N 55 miles — Rd. 204-N 8 miles — CA 198-E 25 miles

Difficulty: 0 of 10
Length: .05 miles
Elevation Change: 0
Water: Yes
Toilets: Yes
Surface: Paved

Best time of year: Summer, since snow arrives in autumn and remains into spring. The lower elevations of Sequoia feature riverside swimming and picnicking.

Along the trail: The parking area is situated among huge sequoia trees, with a natural history museum nearby.

Hazards: None

CHAPTER 19

Lava Crest

TIONESTA

(*Modoc Nation*)
Elevation 6610

The glass climax occurred along a National Forest Service road of ordinary dirt. Flecks of white pumice still litter the road banks, though only a geologist would translate the specks into evidence of the consummation. The plowed lanes roll beneath the car wheels. A sensuous tension holds terrain transcending high ground and approaching the bare essence of our planet.

Graded iron-rich red, the byway winds, a sun streak in a dark fir corridor. A tear in the forest fabric briefly reveals an absolute lapse of landscape – an incident site – but the deep green soon closes the view as the corridor resumes the cooling approach to the spent surfaces – 5, 6,000 feet.

At the top, one of the road's flanks becomes a burnt stone heap and the other a steep mountain's foot. Here on Glass Mountain, California, Earth's hard hands, the casts of a volcanic eruption, are pitched to hold the white of snow in early July. In the mute disarray of the prostrate road flank, we have passed from the quiet of fir forest into the greater quiet of high fir forest and the still greater quiet of a landscape exhausted. Above a layer of forest fire smoke blended of burning fir trees and moss and pine needles, it is quieter than smoke. A primitive silence prevails 900 years after the Earth itself burned.

Along the brittle mannequin of the flank, the planet talks to the mind in random image-making. Objects stand at angles at which they should not stand, chipped and broken like the landscape surrounding them. Colors not proper for the light of the sun bake in sunlight. In piles of gleaming black obsidian, the Earth itself laughs out of turn, a calming laugh, enduring, from deep within itself, and we see the bright smile of stone.

The hike here is self-directed, an inner walk. Bereft of signage, it branches off into wreckage to explore variations of wreckage. Within a crunching obsidian passageway, the eye picks up signals from travelers who place objects along the trail edge to maintain their sense of direction through the 4,210 acres of undefined debris.

The hike traverses a geologic smile of unifying happiness. As the hiker's hours pass inside Earth in this pure air, at a high elevation removed from people and the carbon-laden forest atmospherics, light visits him. This fresh light increasing, the eyes, from pondering this dimension of new creation, squint into a distance that takes in the Blue Ridges, the Canadian Rockies, the Great Smokies, the Atlantic coast, the Pacific coast. Fragrance reaches the light from the smoke layer below arising seemingly from a new Earth still burning. The evidence of creative force unifies East and West, Appalachian and Sierra.

After the AD 1250 eruption, initial life presents itself in bright flashes, like flowers in a vase, to memorialize the great event. Alpine penstemon (*Penstemon davidsonii*) creeps low over the obsidian. A mountain bluebird with hardly a branch to land on flies across the barrenness with the color of pure, clear sky on its back, toward a cluster of whitebark pine (*Pinus albicaulis*) laboring to find nourishment in the incipient earthscape. The sky returns the Earth's smile, touching some of the obsidian pieces with rainbows on their slick surfaces, glossing others with the blue of summer sky.

Across the road on the overseeing mountainside, an intact high ground landscape rises in an even geometry drawn over millions of years, its angle offset with the straight lines of tree trunks. Past a snow patch and into the firs and spruces, the evergreen trunks are erect and broad, and sun beams light silence. This is a giant den, with trees to lean back against, soft needles underfoot, fragrant woodsmoke during the summer fire season. Chunks of obsidian glow like charcoal in the sunny places.

Here, a spiritual mirage overwhelms the diversity of destinations and limitations of distance. A spreading smile invites our footsteps, leads to the eloquent dignity of moss-hung treetrunks and sun-patched silence.

The silent influence led me onward to a high place where this Earth happiness stretches along the roadside like perpetual gleaming snow heaped up. It was a raven's flight from Glass Mountain. I found it when a cowboy with a border collie and hired hand pointed me to a smiling indigenous woman, keeper of the post office and road directions.

When I reached the place she guided me to, I saw that the tree trunks there were statuesque, their boughs stately. The high ground elevated stumps from long-ago logging into memorials of cedars, pines, firs in the shadow/sunlight of deep forest.

Here on the summit of Buck Mountain, above Davis Creek, the flowing lava cooled fastest, first out of Earth, producing a pure obsidian like polished black iron that shone gem-like, some with mahogany mapped out within the black in dialogue with the brown conifer trunks. On the tips of how many indigenous bows did it shine?

I stood beside the car, far above an empty valley studded with sagebrush, beyond pastures and through dust to this place, its recognition initiated by foragers of arrow tips, extended by obsidian miners. The cowboy pulled up in his truck and asked if I had found what I wanted, and I returned his smile. Later,

I read that native people characterized the country around Glass Mountain as "the smiles of God".

The drive back down led into quiet places of wind and bird song; yet behind me, there was a higher silence.

PROFILE

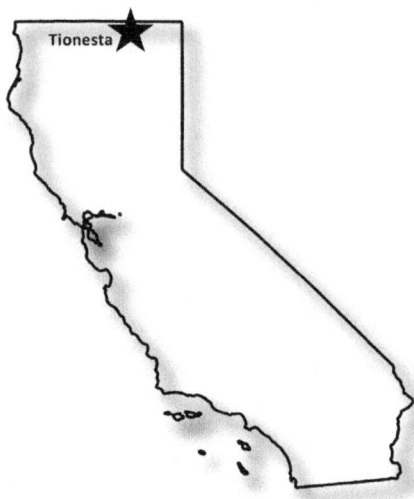

Trip Outline: San Francisco – I 80-E 55 miles — I 505-N 34 miles – I 5-N 126 miles — CA 299-E 89 miles — Bieber Lookout Road 31 miles — CA 139-N 11 miles — Rd. 44 N 01 2 miles

Difficulty: 2 of 10
Length: .05 miles
Elevation Change: 0
Water: No
Toilets: No
Surface: Crushed obsidian

Season: Summer, since the high country snows factor in from October to May

Along the trail: The environs of the path are a vast

archaeological site visited by the Modoc people fashioning weapon tips from obsidian.

Hazards: Getting lost. This environment lacks landmarks. It gives the appearance of an extensive maze. The high altitude would compound matters for a hiker who became disoriented.

CHAPTER 20

Boreal Outcrop

LONE PINE

(Paiute Nation)
Elevation 10100

*T*he trek to the Ancient Forest ascends for 23 miles into very high ground, into a forest established by elevation. A pull-off along the way is named Sierra View. It offers a seminal 100-mile vista of linear high ground featuring the highest mountains in the Lower 48, high enough in the cool atmosphere to sustain patches of white, the Palisades Glaciers, southernmost glaciers in the United States.

Twenty miles ahead, bristlecone pines begin to guard the emptiness, making a pathetic visual statement of extreme tree age, but then a right turn leads to a living work within a perpetual Christmas setting. Conifer boughs shroud the highest visitor center in California, a polished wood/glass gift shop and information area set at the head of a shadowed draw in the landscape. A trail leads into a misshapen tangle of trunks and branches that thousands of years have neglected. The trees silently stand, unitary with slabs of dolomite rock. Visitors from all over the world come to silently stare at these trees, bristlecone pines, oldest trees on earth.

Up here in the thin air, everything moves in slow motion. Behind the visitor center, a path passes a bristlecone pine en route to a 120-year-old nickel mining site that sacrificed many of its kind. A gash mars its bark, but it's not the mark of visitor vandalism. A century-old axe stroke likely made that wound and the slow growth rate of the trees suspended it in time.

A niche species, the bristlecone pine inhabits a topographic apex at the upper limit of tree habitat. The excess elevation immunizes it from climatic law, with each individual living an epochal life enveloping thousands of years of cyclical weather. These trees are glacial relics that participate in a cross-elemental symbiosis. Their ancient roots shield the sharp-sided dolomite rocks occupying this site from erosion; in turn, the rocks feed them underground nutrients.

Pure sunlight, low humidity, wind and unpolluted air foster an extreme conservatism, a willful resistance to age from crown to root. This is the most efficient interface of chlorophyll, wood and mineral on the planet. The age, as well as appearance, of the trunks is unprecedented. They represent the terminal aesthetic of wood: charcoal-black, white, sunset-orange, colors bleeding like paint. The end-state is eerily human, with tortured faces, wounds, arms and legs. Where life deserts them at ground level, indistinct masses lie like prostrate ghosts.

Given such stability within a challenging setting, *Pinus longaeva* offers stiff resistance to climate change, but I followed that universal concept up into these heights to ask Debra Schweitzer, Public Affairs Officer for Inyo National Forest, if staff had documented such change among the storied trees. Her "yes, we have" raised both interest and concern.

She cited a disturbing trend among young bristlecone pines involving their production of resin. They display reduced levels of the sticky substance, which guards the trees by trapping insect prey. Resin is also the means by which the species copes with intense dryness, allowing it to achieve longevity. The altered level reflects altered climate, portending shorter tree lifespans.

Downslope, an introduced fungus, whitebark pine blister rust, worries Schweitzer, since the bristlecone pine bears an ecological relation to whitebark pine. Staff have not witnessed an incursion yet, but "we are watching," she said.

Matthew Salzer, Research Associate at the Arizona Tree Ring Lab and co-author of a paper on bristlecone pine ecology published in the Proceedings of the National Academy of Sciences, finds the signature of climate change at the high border zone known as tree line. There, bristlecones exhibit a burst of growth, expressed through an increase in tree ring width unprecedented in 3,500 years. The paper's research eliminates possible causes one by one and arrives at a correlation with higher temperatures symptomatic of climate change.

A primal display of climate change punctuates a hike along the North Fork of Big Pine Creek near the Ancient Forest. Hikers viewing the Palisades Glaciers compare their white contours with historic photos and realize they are viewing mini-glaciers reduced by global warming.

The Schulman Grove behind the visitor center contains individual pines aged 3-4,000 years, with a known maximum exceeding 5,000, and sees over 30,000 visitors annually, but the surrounding area is free of heavy restrictions, allowing independent quests for insight. I took a hike into a signage-free stand directly east of the touristed area, where I enjoyed an unfettered experience with the trees. I walked slowly in the high altitude, crossing a barren meadow of a post-glacial valley, working upwards among the trunks, boreal birds and wildflowers, knowing that the bristlecones had written a statement about life.

I looked at the pines under the blue pane of sky and saw a stark mirror of humanity. The dead crowns formed polished heads rounded by time. They died but didn't die: Antique wood sprouted green life from parchment-toned wood grain. They paralleled us; and in this, the bristlecones graced these highest places with a generational kinship.

PROFILE

Trip Outline: 101-N 10 miles — CA 170-N 6 miles — I 5-N 9 miles — CA 14-N 183 miles – CA 168-E 13 miles — White Mountain Road 10 miles

Difficulty: 3 of 10
Length: 1.0 miles
Elevation Change: 280
Surface: Dirt/stone

Best time of year: Summer, due to high elevation snows

Along the trail: Interpretive signs and benches. Meadows away from the visitor center offer convenient access to alpine wildflowers.

Hazards: Rocky trail; and for the susceptible, high altitude

About the Author

Bill Rozday

B ill Rozday worked as an editor in Washington, D.C. but grew up in Pennsylvania, walking to the school bus through the woods past his Ukrainian grandfather's frame house. The trail through the woods eventually joined trails in Wales, British Columbia; and finally, California.

INDEX

V

W

X

Y

Z

Made in the USA
Middletown, DE
05 December 2023